CONTENTS

Acknowledgments

Telling the story of the oldest prison in Kansas cannot be done by one person. There are numerous people who have added their input to create this book. In my eight years as Lansing Historical Museum site supervisor, on the Lansing Correctional Facility grounds, I have acquired what I call my LCF family. I look out for their history, and they look out for me. Brett Peterson, Lansing Correctional Facility public information officer, answered my countless prison questions. Phil White, Lansing Correctional Facility media production director, provided additional photographs. Chaplain Don Almond and Renda Craft answered questions about religion in the prison. The staff at Kansas Correctional Industries in Lansing, including Debra Gillespie and Doug Friez, provided invaluable information.

Jeremy Barclay, public affairs director of the Kansas Department of Corrections Central Office, also answered questions and offered support. John Cooling, Ed Simons, David McKune, Steve Jansen, Gene Young, Peggy Howard, and Gail Banker Armstrong provided historical insight and photographs of the Lansing Correctional Facility. The staff of the Leavenworth Public Library and Sally York of the Miners Hall Museum assisted in the research component of the book. I would like to thank Arcadia Publishing editors Lydia Rollins and Jesse Darland for giving us the opportunity to share our history with the world through this project.

I would like to thank the members of the Lansing Historical Society who have worked many years to preserve the history of Lansing and supported me during my tenure. I would also like to thank my father, Samuel Phillippi, and my aunt, Virginia Aubert, for their love and support over the years. Both have fostered and encouraged my interest in history from an early age. I would also like to thank my friends Cheryl and Keith Baranow, Katie Herrick, and Christina Moberly for their support during this project. Finally, I would like to thank the city of Lansing for giving me the opportunity to preserve and educate others about the unique history of Lansing, Kansas.

Unless otherwise noted, all images appear courtesy of the Lansing Historical Museum.

INTRODUCTION

Built in 1868, the Lansing Correctional Facility (LCF) is the oldest prison in Kansas, predating Lansing, Kansas, by a decade. Once known as the Kansas State Penitentiary (KSP), the prison has seen many changes in corrections and the surrounding area. For years, Lansing remained a small community, until incorporation in 1959. Since then, it has grown to over 11,000 residents.

The prison itself has gone through good times and bad. The early days focused more on punishment than rehabilitation of inmates. The Kansas Department of Correction's mission statement is "a safer Kansas through effective correctional services." The Lansing Correctional Facility utilizes outside programs, such as Reaching Out From Within, Brothers In Blue Reentry, Arts in Prison, and the Safe Harbor Prison Dog Program to further the rehabilitation of inmates and reduce recidivism.

Interpreting the prison's history is not an easy task. It can elicit various emotions for those from all walks of life. Some people have relatives who were victims of crime. Families of inmates often suffer because of the crime their relatives have committed. The issue of capital punishment raises passionate arguments from individuals and groups who are for or against it. I have respect for the victims of crimes and the family members of inmates. I also have an obligation to educate the public about our history.

Yes, between May 6, 1950, and June 22, 1965, ten men were hanged at the prison for their crimes. The best-known pair—Richard Hickock and Perry Smith—were featured in Truman Capote's book *In Cold Blood* and have been portrayed in at least three movies. They are buried at Mount Muncie Cemetery in Lansing. In December 2012, their remains were exhumed to collect samples for DNA analysis. Law enforcement officials in Florida were trying to link the pair to the killings of a family of four in 1959, but the results were inconclusive because the samples had degraded over time.

We acknowledge this chapter of the prison's history, but we do not actively promote it out of respect to the remaining members of the Clutter family and the citizens of Holcomb, who still feel the effects of the tragedy even after 55 years. Prison officials are adamant that we do not glorify what the inmates have done. It is not ethical for us to glorify the crimes committed by inmates.

The photographs in this book were selected from hundreds among the collections of the Lansing Historical Museum, the Lansing Correctional Facility, and local citizens. When selecting a photograph, I used a set of criteria to determine whether to incorporate it. The photographs that were selected have something to add to telling the story of the Lansing Correctional Facility. With so few photographs of the women's prison (now East Unit), I was limited in what I could share.

While the word *prison* evokes negative thoughts for many people, there are also positive attributes of the prison that are often overlooked. This book features information on the prison's past and present industries, from the coal mine to the Kansas Correctional Industries metals division. Motorists on Kansas highways see the results of inmates' labor every day. The Kansas Department of Transportation and Kansas Turnpike Authority use the paint made at the Lansing Correctional Facility to line the roads. Many of the traffic signs are also made at Lansing.

The farm nestled against the banks of the mighty Missouri River continues to raise livestock and grow crops. If the prison pumpkin patch has a good season, inmates deliver a pumpkin to each student at the Sheldon Child Development Center in Topeka, as well as local Lansing and Leavenworth schools. In a good year, the inmates distribute approximately 1,000 pumpkins as part of their community service project.

The photographs herein offer a glimpse into life behind the walls. They show the living arrangements for different custody levels, from single cells to dormitory style. Over the years, buildings have changed, been added, or destroyed. The castle tops no longer adorn the original building, and in February 2009, a red metal roof was installed. The old medical clinic was demolished to make way for a new clinic, providing better care for inmates and a safer environment for the clinic staff.

In June 1969, a violent riot and the subsequent wave of arson fires, self-mutilation, and violence against fellow inmates rocked the Kansas State Penitentiary. Some of these instances were fatal. Photographs reveal what officers have discovered during shakedowns at the prison, including drugs and weapons.

An image not featured in this book shows the stab wound Lt. D. Myers received on August 29, 1969, after being attacked by an inmate. In the history of the penitentiary, seven staff members have lost their lives in the line of duty. Every May, the Lansing Correctional Facility holds a memorial service to remember these men.

The Lansing Correctional Facility predates what is now the Hutchinson Correctional Facility by 27 years. Prior to the institution at Hutchinson, juvenile offenders were thrown in with the adult inmates at Lansing. The chances for rehabilitating these young offenders dwindled due to the influence of adult criminals.

Today, the Kansas Department of Corrections encompasses several facilities: Lansing Correctional Facility, 1868; Kansas Juvenile Correctional Complex, 1879; Hutchinson Correctional Facility, 1895; Topeka Correctional Facility, 1960; Larned Juvenile Correctional Facility, 1971; Winfield Correctional Facility, 1984; Norton Correctional Facility, 1987; Ellsworth Correctional Facility, 1989; El Dorado Correctional Facility, 1991; and Larned Correctional Mental Health Facility, 1992.

The following are satellite units of correctional facilities in Kansas: Wichita Work Release Facility (Winfield Correctional Facility), 1976; Norton Correctional Facility East Unit in Stockton, 1989; and El Dorado Correctional Facility Southeast Unit in Oswego, 2013. The Lansing Correctional Facility had its own satellite, Lansing Correctional Facility South Unit in Osawatomie, but due to budget cuts in April 2009, this unit was repurposed and transferred to the Kansas Department of Aging and Disability Services.

Together, these institutions work to keep the public safe and to rehabilitate inmates during their incarceration. Since over 90 percent of inmates will eventually be released, it is critical to invest resources to rehabilitate them so they do not reoffend.

In my eight years of studying prison history, I have found that I look at the world differently. I hope this book will give readers a new perspective on the history of the Lansing Correctional Facility and the role of corrections in our community.

One

THE OLDEST PRISON IN KANSAS

The Lansing Correctional Facility is the oldest prison in Kansas. Originally known as the Kansas State Penitentiary, the Kansas legislature changed the institution's name to Lansing Correctional Facility on June 18, 1990. Architect Erasmus Carr, who designed the Kansas capitol building, drew the plans for the Kansas State Penitentiary based on the prison in Joliet, Illinois.

It is also the largest prison in the Kansas Department of Corrections (KDOC). The prison's two main units are Central Unit and East Unit. Central Unit includes an 11-acre facility for maximum-security inmates and a 46-acre medium-security facility. East Unit, located on Kansas Highway 5, consists of an 85-acre facility to house minimum-security inmates. LCF is also home to one of two centers in KDOC's transportation system to move inmates to other Kansas correctional facilities. The prison has a capacity of 2,405 inmates.

The community of Lansing has grown around the prison, and the prison grounds are home to the Leavenworth County Fire District No. 1 fire station and the Lansing Historical Museum.

Leavenworth County wanted to have the state prison because it would be good for the local economy. Gov. Charles Robinson delayed its construction, hoping to relocate the prison to where it would benefit him. However, the county persevered, and after a delay due to the Civil War, the first inmates were moved from temporary quarters into the new prison in July 1868. From January 1, 1867, to July 1, 1882, there were 3,019 prisoners who did time in Lansing.

This 1920s–1930s drawing of the Kansas State Penitentiary has several features that no longer exist. The bandstand provided a place for the penitentiary band to perform for the community. Lifelong resident Eugene Young remembers listening to concerts on the prison lawn. The tracks transported shale from the prison coal mine to the ravine on the west end of the prison grounds to be used as fill.

On November 7, 1916, a new electric motor attached to the ventilation fan caused a fire that sent clouds of smoke into the North Wing cells. Officer A.C. Taylor single-handedly had to open each cell to let the inmates out to safety. Inmate firefighters, along with Leavenworth firefighters, fought the blaze that heavily damaged the roof, fan room, and north end of the cell tiers.

Inmates are pictured here using scaffolding. In 1928, warden W.H. Mackey reported on construction projects at the prison to deal with an increase in staff and inmates. In April 1927, construction began to rebuild the South Wing Cell House, which was a dark, damp, and unsanitary building. The brick was made at the prison, the lumber was harvested from the island farm, and the stone for concrete was from the shale pit quarry.

The Kansas State Penitentiary had a fountain near the main building, as depicted in this postcard mailed to Mrs. S.M. Chamberlain in Kansas City, Kansas, on August 14, 1913. Native to tropical Polynesia and southeastern Asia, elephant-ear plants are also visible in the foreground. Written on the back of the postcard was the following message: "Dear Everybody, Well, we just arrived here a few minutes ago. All for now. From Linnet C."

This early penitentiary greenhouse was used to grow plants for the prison grounds. When resident Eugene Young was about 10 years old, his parents would let him visit with a "trusty," who taught Young how to transplant flowers and care for them. His parents never worried about him talking to an inmate. Today, inmate work crews take care of the numerous flower beds at the prison.

In 1890, John Reynolds published his book *The Twin Hells* in which he described life in the penitentiary. His cell measured four feet wide, seven feet long, and seven feet high. Two iron bed racks folded up flat against the wall, and the pillow and bedtick were stuffed with corn husks. A tin bucket with water, a washbasin, a short broom, chair, and Bible rounded out the cell's furnishings.

LCF's cells have evolved through the years. In the D Cell House, for example, cells have a woven mesh to prevent people from reaching out of or into them. Inmates in wheelchairs have modified doors so there is enough clearance for the wheelchair to pass through the opening. However, the cells are not air-conditioned. Fans are used in the summer, and the inmates have access to ice and water to help them stay cool.

This Kansas State Penitentiary storeroom was built in 1879. Today, the prison uses several Quonset huts to store equipment and materials. In 2007, when the Lansing Historical Museum had a fire, the prison stored museum items in a Quonset hut while the museum underwent renovations. These prefabricated galvanized-steel buildings were inspired by the Nissen huts developed by the British in World War I.

What could be mistaken for a downtown area of a small Kansas town was actually a section within the walls of the Kansas State Penitentiary. In many ways, the largest prison in the Kansas Department of Corrections is like a small town, with approximately 2,400 inmates and over 1,000 regular and contract staff members. Out of the 626 incorporated Kansas towns, 88 percent have a population less than 3,400.

A KSP truck is pictured with the prison water tower in the distance. Among the vehicles used to carry out various tasks at the prison are pickup trucks for security patrols, as well as for supervisors to inspect work detail projects. Old school buses have been transformed into a type of bus/pickup hybrid. The open half of the bus provides space to carry lawnmowers and tools, while the enclosed half carries the inmates.

The Kansas State Penitentiary deputy warden's office is the circular building at left in the background. It was known as the bell tower because of the bell on top that officials used to signal the inmates. Today, the Lansing Correctional Facility has three deputy wardens: Colette Winkelbauer, deputy warden of operations; Bill Shipman, deputy warden of support services; and Shannon Meyer, deputy warden of programs.

In the autumn of 1969, inmates began installing a 12-foot chain-link fence to enclose the front yard of the Kansas State Penitentiary. The $12,500 project included an electrically operated gate at Tower 1 and the main entrance, as well as two utility gates for vehicle access. Over 730 feet of fence was used and trimmed with barbwire. Floodlights were installed for nighttime security.

Inmates are allowed visits on a rotating schedule. Visitors must abide by a number of rules. Items such as tobacco, cell phones, and pocket knives are prohibited. For security, staff stamps the hands of visitors with a special ink that glows under a black light. To purchase snack items during visitation, people exchange money for special tokens for the vending machines.

This 1960s photograph shows the area west of the original prison building. Since incorporation in 1959, Lansing's population has grown dramatically. In 1960, the population of Lansing stood at 1,261. By 2010, it had risen to 11,265. Today, there are fewer buildings on the west lawn, including a fire station, the Lansing Historical Museum, a parole office, and a former day care building.

Kansas Avenue was once lined with housing for the staff of the penitentiary. All but two of the houses were demolished. One is currently the parole office, and until 2013, the other housed Safe Kids Day Care. In 1989, the demolition of the Santa Fe Railroad depot appeared eminent. LCF offered a site for the building, which was moved in 1992 and now houses the Lansing Historical Museum.

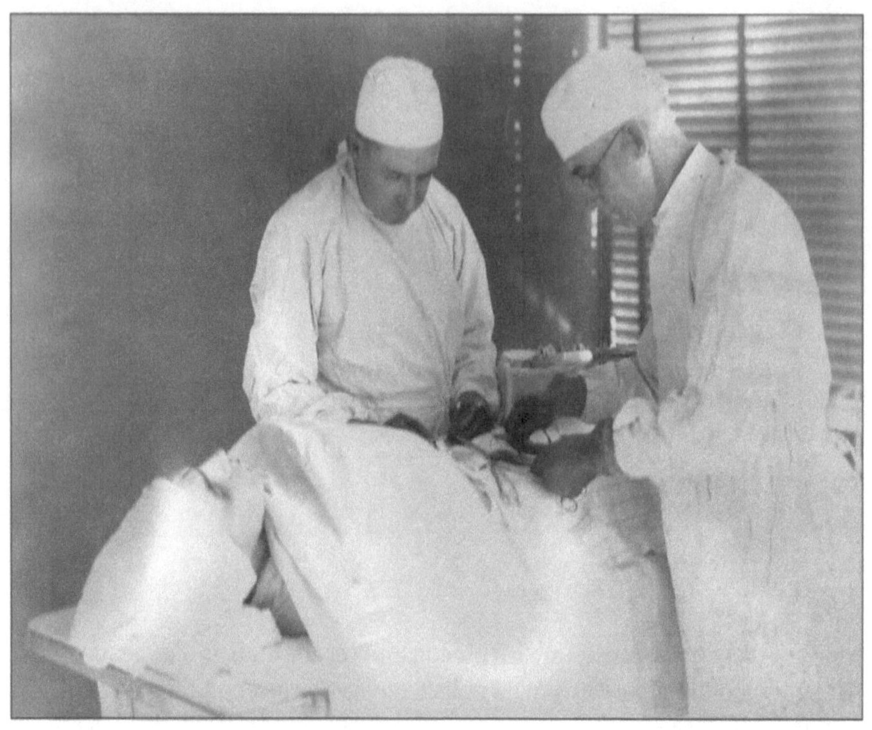

Dr. Sherman Axford (right) performs an operation on an inmate in the 1920s. Today, surgical cases are sent to area hospitals. In 2010, LCF opened a new two-story, 48-bed clinic at a cost of $5.5 million. By using inmate labor, the clinic cost less than half of what it would have with outside labor. The new clinic features dialysis machines, which saves LCF from having to transport inmates outside the walls for treatments.

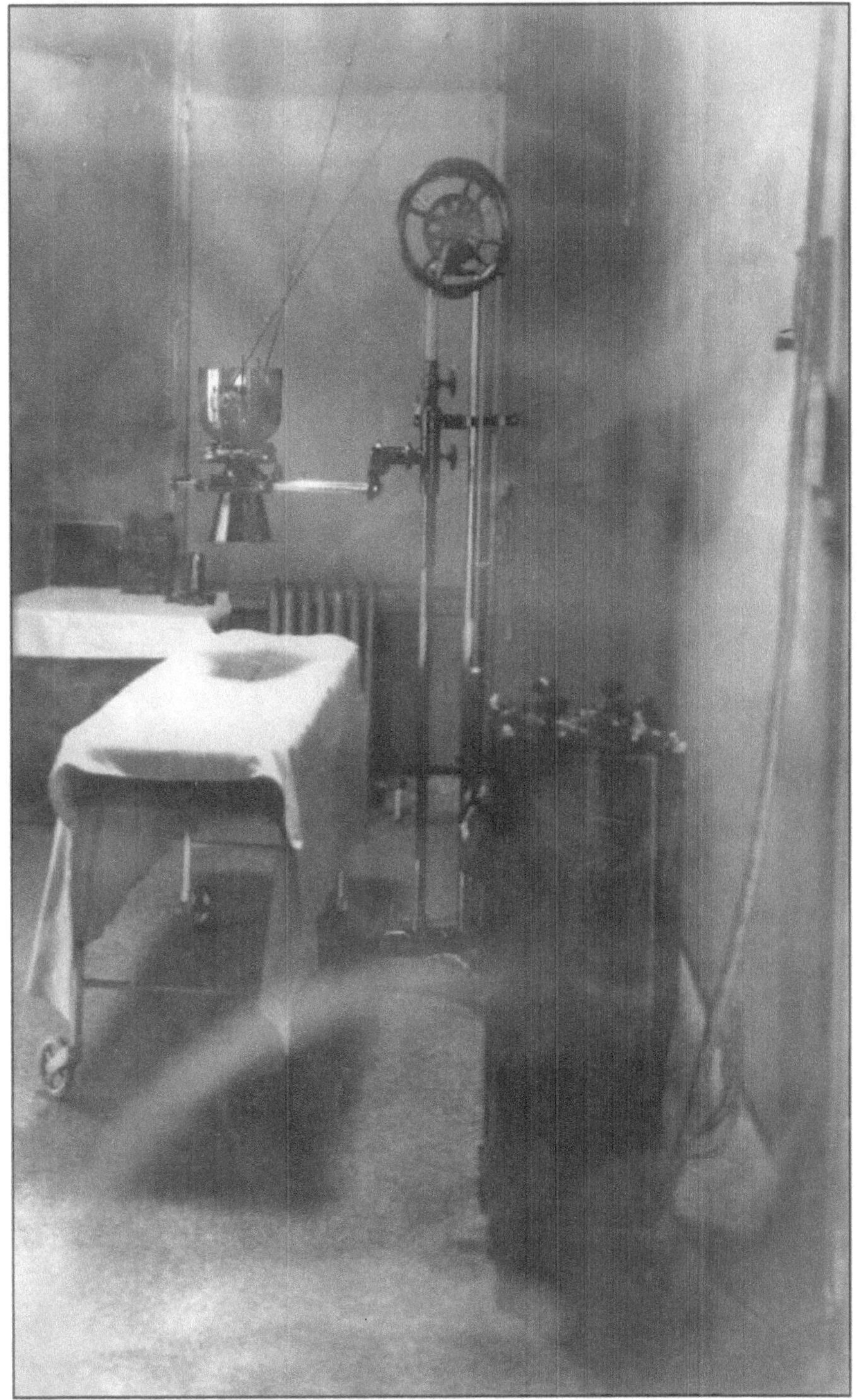

Here is an X-ray machine at the Kansas State Penitentiary in the 1920s. While the new clinic at the Lansing Correctional Facility provides treatment for many medical issues, including chronic illnesses like diabetes, high blood pressure, and arthritis, inmates with broken bones must be sent to area hospitals. Two officers are required to accompany an inmate to the hospital. As wards of the state, inmates are guaranteed health care services.

Rebuilt in August 1958, Dock 2 is one of the few vehicle access points into the Lansing Correctional Facility. The dock is used to bring in construction machinery, supplies, fire trucks, and ambulances. Vehicles are searched before entering the prison and again when they leave. Officers look for contraband items such as cell phones, knives, guns, and narcotics, or even inmates themselves hiding in the vehicles. The rail track visible below no longer exists. The tracks in the area of Kansas Avenue and Helen Street in Lansing were removed in the early 1980s.

Staff members were unable to find any information about this photograph, labelled "Fish House—Early 1940s." Perhaps inmates caught fish from the Missouri River to sell or use in the prison.

An old visitation room is seen here in the 1950s. The partition running along the table prevented visitors from passing contraband. Today, due to space, only four visitors can visit an inmate at a time. A person is allowed on only one inmate's visitation list, except when inmates and visitors are immediate family. Today, physical interaction for a contact visit is limited to a brief embrace and kiss.

An officer in the old cage area pictured here had control of the sally port to the waiting room. Today's heavy sally port doors, with a narrow slit of a window, are moved with the touch of a button. Those passing through have to wait for the first door to close before the second one will open.

As punishment, disruptive Kansas State Penitentiary inmates were sent to the windowless Adjustment and Treatment Building, which was constructed in the 1960s. The slang term for the building was "the hole." In the summer of 1991, the building ceased to house segregation inmates, and was remodeled as the Treatment and Reintegration Unit (TRU), with the addition of windows and improvement of the ventilation and lighting systems. This is the prison's transitional mental health unit. (Courtesy of Gail Banker Armstrong.)

These photographs show what life was like inside the Adjustment and Treatment Building, with no windows and no television or radio. It appears that the inmate of the cell below had reading materials available, but little else to pass the time. The toilet and sink are made of metal, which prevents an inmate from breaking off pieces to make a weapon. (Courtesy of Gail Banker Armstrong.)

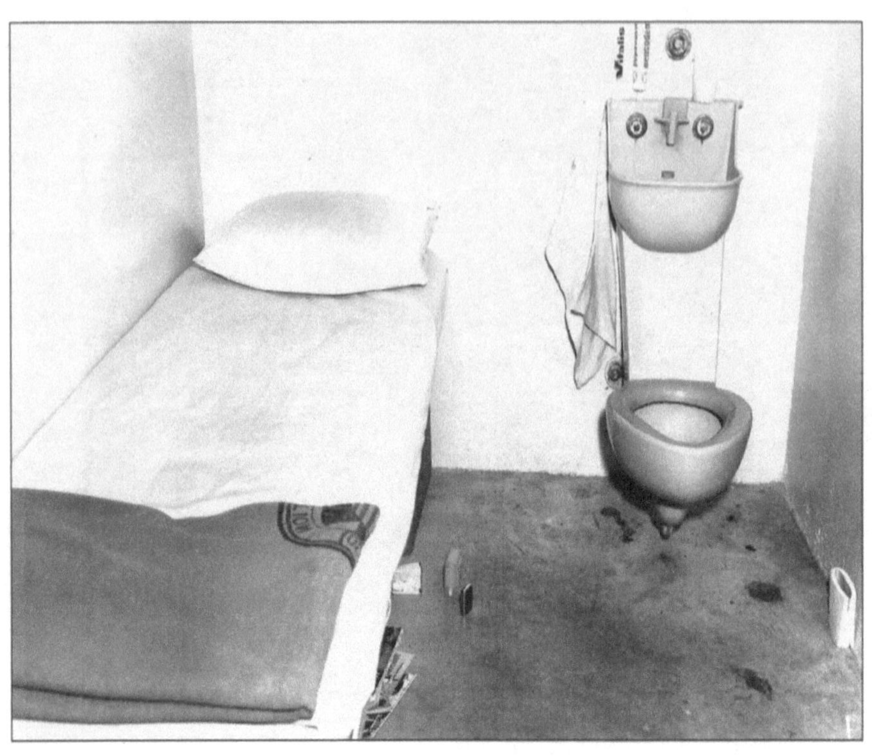

This 1950s photograph shows inmates modernizing Tower 3, located next to Dock 2, near Kansas Avenue. Officers in the tower vigilantly patrol for anything suspicious or out of the ordinary. The officers observe the comings and goings of visitors and vehicles to make sure they do not attempt to throw contraband over the wall or leave it on the grounds where a work crew inmate can find it.

Made from either sandstone or limestone, the prison walls are at least 15 feet high, 6 feet wide at the base, and approximately 4 feet wide at the top. The seasonal freeze-thaw cycle takes a toll on the walls, which require periodic repair work. The prison later added chain link fencing and razor wire as an escape deterrent.

This photograph is believed to show the demolition of the old Segregation and Isolation Building, which served as death row for many years. As of January 2014, nine inmates were on state death row in Kansas, most of whom were kept at the El Dorado Correctional Facility. One was assigned to Lansing because several people who work at El Dorado knew the inmate's victim. Victims' rights play an important role in the correctional system.

Known as the Service Building, this is the largest structure inside the walls of the Lansing Correctional Facility. Utilized for a variety of purposes, the building contains a dining area, kitchen, gymnasium, chapel, the Education Department, and offices for re-entry staff. Disciplinary hearings are held in this facility, which also housed the medical clinic until the new clinic was built. The Service Building has never housed inmates.

Kansas State Penitentiary inmates demolish the old Segregation and Isolation Building. A precursor to the Adjustment and Treatment Building, this facility was used to house inmates who required separation from the general population for serious infractions. The century-old structure was torn down in 1970 to make room for the proposed All Faiths Chapel. The 1969 Kansas legislature approved the construction of the chapel on the condition that the estimated $100,000 in construction costs was raised privately. The chapel was never built.

Deputy warden J.J. Banker monitors the serving line in the dining hall. Between meals, inmates can purchase snack items from the canteen. In 2009, inmates published the *Gumbo Cookbook*, featuring dishes made from items available in the canteen. The recipe for gumbo pizza calls for eight packages of Ramen noodles, eight soups, and two bags of tortilla chips or a box of cheese crackers to make the crust. (Courtesy of Gail Banker Armstrong.)

Preparing three meals a day for 2,400 inmates is quite an undertaking. Variables include inmates who have religious or medically restricted diets. It costs $1,585.15 a year to feed an inmate at LCF. Currently, the prison contracts with Aramark for food service, and those employees supervise the inmates who work in the kitchen.

For decades, the LCF dining hall had long tables, until warden Sherman Crouse changed the seating layout to four-person tables in the 1960s. Inmates who need specialized meals because of their religious beliefs are required to fill out paperwork and meet with a chaplain to explain their reasoning for a specific diet. If the diet is approved, the inmate is issued a new identification badge that includes either "VEG" for vegetarian or "REL" for religious diet. Inmates with medical issues that necessitate a modified diet also receive a special badge.

A Kansas State Penitentiary inmate band performs for their fellow inmates in the prison gymnasium. In the background are murals that were painted by inmates. Murals can be found at various locations throughout the prison.

The murals in the gymnasium depict life in Kansas when immigrants looking for a new home traveled by covered wagon across the prairie. In the background, behind the covered wagon, is a herd of buffalo. The American bison, commonly referred to as a buffalo, is the official state animal of Kansas. Buffalo are also featured in the first line of the state song, "Home on the Range." (Courtesy of Phil White, LCF.)

There were as many as 300 minimum-custody men assigned to Dormitory 2 at "the Farm." In addition to two military-style dormitories, the farm included indoor-outdoor visitation areas and a recreation building with weight-lifting equipment, Ping-Pong tables, card tables, a basketball court, a track, and a baseball field. Inmate work details were dispatched five days a week throughout the community, while some assignments took place on the prison grounds, in the garden, or at the Kansas Correctional Industries.

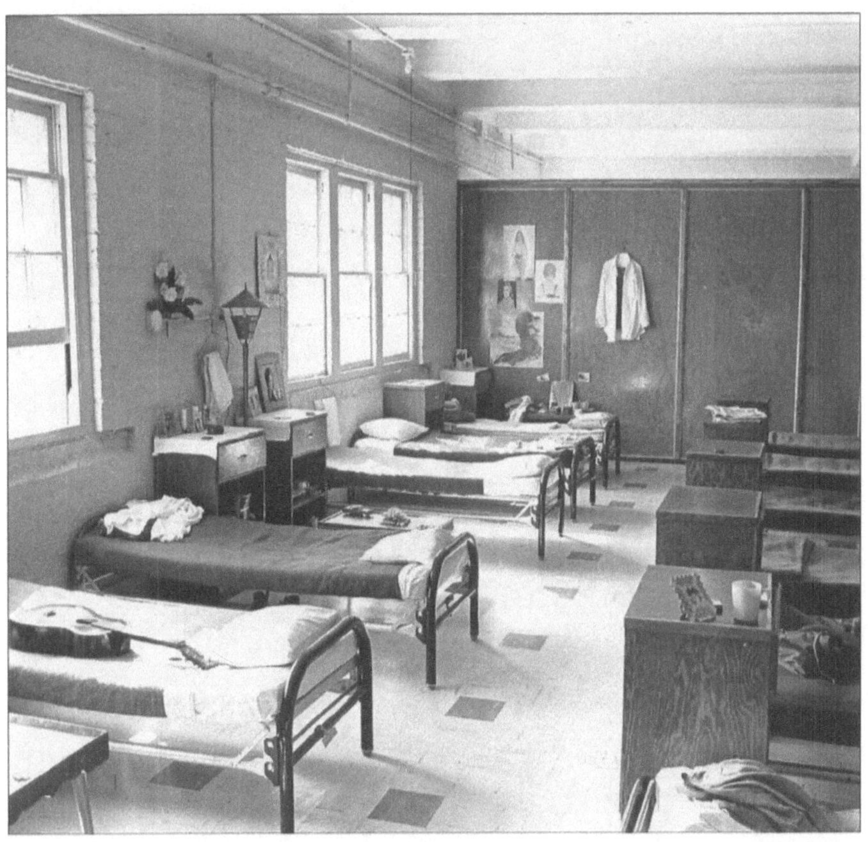

The inmates on the Farm were occasionally evacuated due to flooding. In July 1991, the Farm was closed due to a court order from Judge Rodgers. One year later, much of the Farm was swept away during flooding of the Missouri River. Today, all maximum-custody inmates are kept in single-person cells. Medium- and minimum-custody inmates are more likely to be found in multi-occupancy units, such as four-person cells, two-person rooms, or dormitories.

Construction projects on the grounds of the oldest penitentiary in Kansas can lead to some surprises. In 2008, workers discovered a "monster hole," measuring approximately 20 feet deep, 40–50 feet long, and 20–25 feet wide, while working on the site of the new infirmary. Officials believe it was a cistern to store water. (Courtesy of LCF.)

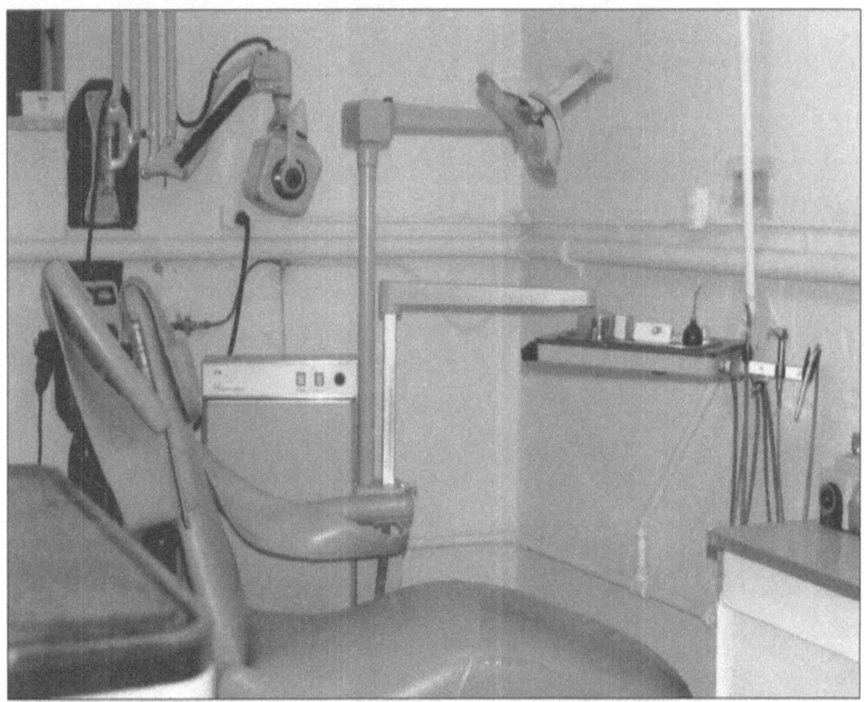

All inmates have access to dental care while incarcerated. According to the *Twentieth Biennial Report of the Board of Penal Institutions*, between July 1, 1954, and June 30, 1956, dentist Dr. Walter Cyhel reported 3,480 teeth extractions, 2,188 amalgam fillings, 487 porcelain fillings, 1,238 gum treatments, 240 dentures built, 520 dentures repaired, and 493 X-rays done.

Pictured here is Christmas caroling at J.J and Virgie Banker's state house on Kansas Avenue on the prison grounds. The Banker family had an inmate assigned to them to do chores such as mowing the lawn. (Courtesy of Gail Banker Armstrong.)

Corrections specialist Luisa Mangieri (center) and corrections officer Peggy Teeters (right) are seen here at a meeting. For 101 years, the penitentiary was staffed by only men. In December 1969, the prison hired eight women for clerical work, partly due to a shortage of male clerks. Gail Banker Armstrong worked at KSP from 1972 to 1974 on the third floor of the main building. During that time, she said few women went inside the prison.

Canines in the Safe Harbor Prison Dog adoption program live with their handlers in the cells and dormitories at the Lansing Correctional Facility. This program gives the dogs much needed socialization, and many inmates enjoy having the opportunity to pet and play with the dogs. (Courtesy of LCF.)

One of the Safe Harbor Prison Dogs trots down the passage of a cell house in the Lansing Correctional Facility. The Safe Harbor Prison Dog adoption program has rescued several dogs from other agencies that were displaced as a result of Hurricane Katrina, as well as tornado disasters in Joplin, Missouri, and Moore, Oklahoma. (Courtesy of LCF.)

Corrections specialist Jeffery Carroll and his partner, Bart, practice searching for contraband in the K-9 Unit. The prison has replicas of the areas that a K-9 commonly searches so the dog is accustomed to the environment. Today, there are four dogs in the K-9 Unit: Bart, King, Beyonce, and Hobbie. Their breeds are either Belgian Malinois or German shepherd. The dogs are rewarded with praise and their favorite toy when they find contraband items. (Author's collection.)

Carroll uses the Lansing Correctional Facility's K-9 obstacle course to hone the skills of the dogs in his command. The sole purpose of LCF's dogs is to detect contraband. Once the dog has found the packet of drugs during a training exercise, the container holding the drugs must be aired out. The dogs are also being used to uncover contraband cell phones. (Author's collection.)

When inmates pass away, their loved ones have the option of claiming the remains for burial. If unclaimed, the prison has the remains cremated. The staff holds a small service for the deceased and interns the ashes at the prison cemetery, sometimes referred to as Cemetery of the Good Thief. After interning inmates at Mount Muncie Cemetery for many years, LCF resumed interning inmates on the prison grounds in 1996.

The Lansing Correctional Facility encompasses 142 acres of land in downtown Lansing. Over the years, the prison has been a good neighbor to the community. Its farming operations near the Missouri River comprise 1,900 acres. The city of Lansing leases land from the prison for the wastewater treatment facility and Lost 80 Park.

Two

WORKING THE LAND

Since the beginning, agriculture has played an important role in Kansas, and the prison is no exception. With access to the fertile farmland bordering the Missouri River, the inmates raised livestock and crops to feed the prison population. Over the years, the inmates have raised cattle, pigs, chickens, turkeys, and goats. Through manual and mechanized labor, the farm grew garden vegetables and crops such as corn, tobacco, alfalfa, oats, wheat, milo, soybeans, straw, and cane.

Currently, the prison farm raises cattle and grows corn and soybeans. The herd has 70 adult female cows, and the steers are sold in the autumn. The farm plants 1,600 acres, with 700 for corn and 800 for soybeans. The cattle operation covers 300 acres of pasture and pens. The Kansas Correctional Industries employs two civilians as farm manager and assistant farm manager. Currently, six Lansing Correctional Facility inmates, some of whom come from farming backgrounds, work the land. The inmates till, produce hay, mow, repair fences, cut brush, and cut firewood, which is sold to the public. Some of the inmates who are released go on to find agricultural jobs. The farm has tractors in several different sizes; however, they currently have to hire out custom harvesting jobs that require the use of combines.

In 1916, the farm consisted of almost 700 acres of highland and 1,300 acres of low island land in the Missouri River. C.L. Dews, superintendent of the prison farm, reported growing 190 acres of corn, 45 acres of potatoes, 10 acres of watermelons, 10 acres of alfalfa, 60 acres of cane, 20 acres of garden stuff, 8 acres of sweet potatoes, and 6 acres of tobacco.

Before the widespread mechanization of farming, the Kansas State Penitentiary relied on mules to pull machinery and loads. In the *Twentieth Biennial Report of the Kansas State Penitentiary*, superintendent C.L. Dews noted, "To operate this farm we are using three yoke of oxen, eighteen head of mules, one horse, and the necessary equipment and machinery to carry on the work."

In 1956, farm superintendent J.N. Bieri noted that, in two years, the Kansas State Penitentiary farm had grown 82,553 pounds of cantaloupe at a value of $1,730.06. The farm also grew 392,265 pounds of watermelon worth $7,845.30. The farm grew 36 types of crops that were worth $200,623.10. Food from the farm was used to feed the inmates. The man in the photograph is possibly warden Kirk Prather.

The prison fashioned sticks into tomato stakes to support the plants at the penitentiary farm. According to the *Twentieth Biennial Report of the Board of Penal Institutions*, the prison grew 78,814 pounds of tomatoes worth $1,576.28. In the same report, Omar A. Huey, cannery superintendent, reported the production of 1,018 No. 10 cans of ketchup, 995 cans of juice, 244 cans of puree, and 617 cans of whole tomatoes.

The Kansas State Penitentiary farm raised stock and dairy cattle. In 1956, J.N. Bieri reported that, in the stock herd, there were 26 cows, 55 yearlings, and 85 calves. The bull had died. The dairy herd had three bulls, 94 cows, 26 heifers, and 31 calves. A heifer is a cow that has not had a calf.

Shown here is the milking barn at the Kansas State Penitentiary. Dairy cows have to be milked twice a day. In the *Twentieth Biennial Report of Board of Penal Institutions*, the prison dairy herd produced 227,952 gallons of milk and cream. The milk and cream, worth a 25¢ a gallon, was valued at $56,908.68.

On July 1, 1954, the Kansas State Penitentiary had six boars, 158 brood sows, 67 shoats, 455 fat hogs, 597 pigs, and 20 gilts. The sows gave birth to 2,404 piglets that year. Shoats are pigs that have been weaned, fat hogs are raised for meat, pigs refer to piglets still nursing, and gilts are female pigs that have not given birth.

In 1954, Bess Ballard reported in the *Nineteenth Biennial Report of the State Industrial Farm for Women* that they had raised "poultry, fryers, fat hens, and turkeys to supply our tables with poultry twice a week." The turkeys were started in May and ready for the table in autumn. The Kansas State Penitentiary also raised turkeys to provide food for the inmates.

Female inmates are working the field in Lansing. Inmates often take great pride in their work. At the Kansas State Industrial Farm for Women in 1954, Bess Ballard reported, "We do take pride in our daily work and take time to look out over God's beautiful hills; being thankful that we have such beautiful surroundings in which to work."

Tractors like this one replaced the steel plow that had worked the Kansas prairie for years. Farmers could plant more crop acreage faster with tractors and did not need to rely on draft horses, mules, or oxen to work the fields. This development permanently altered the agricultural landscape. Today's tractors use GPS to complete tilling, planting, spraying, and harvesting tasks more efficiently.

The waters of the Missouri River provided fertile land for the Kansas State Penitentiary's farm operations; however, flooding spelled disaster for crops located close to the river. This photograph shows flooded fields and sandbags lining the road to prevent the floodwaters from causing structural failure of the road.

This suspension bridge crossed the Missouri River, where it connected to the prison's property. It appears that the bridge is either under construction or possibly being repaired from flood damage. There is a railroad crossing on the far side of the bridge and what appears to be a corn crop in the foreground. The photograph is from 1931 or 1932. (Courtesy of the LCF.)

Occasionally, inmates from the women's prison wandered away from the grounds. In 1950, Frank Hartig, 69, recaptured Mary Jane Chawkley, 24, and Lois Lemoyne, 22. Chawkley was serving time for smuggling a hacksaw blade to four inmates who had escaped from the Johnson County Jail in Olathe. Interestingly, Hartig, a special Wyandotte County sheriff's deputy, captured two of the men Chawkley had helped escape.

In 1926, the wife of one of the inmates who worked in the prison cornfield snuck into the farmland and stashed a bottle of morphine for her husband to find. She marked the location by securing a ribbon to a cornstalk. Deputy warden R.H. Hudspeth arrested Imogene Williams on a road near the prison dairy farm, and she was sent to the Leavenworth County Jail.

Three

PRISON INDUSTRIES

Industries such as the prison coal mine and twine plant create revenue, allowing the penitentiary to become more self-sufficient. The industries also provide inmates an opportunity to earn wages and gain job experience. In 1957, the Kansas legislature passed the Prison Made Goods Act, which created Kansas Correctional Industries (KCI). Kansas Correctional Industries employs over 1,100 inmates in traditional and private-sector jobs.

Kansas Correctional Industries at Lansing has five divisions: chemical products, data entry, metal products, LCF agri-business, and KCI's main warehouse and distribution hub. In order for a private industry to use inmate labor, it must show the jobs cannot be filled by the general public. Inmates must use their wages to pay for restitution, child support, 25 percent of their room and board, and funds placed in a mandatory savings account. Inmates without restitution or other court obligations pay a percentage into the crime victim's fund. Upon release, the inmate has access to the savings account to assist them in re-entering life outside the walls. Inmates working in the industries have fewer disciplinary problems and a reduced recidivism rate.

The penitentiary's industrial area is shown here in the early 1900s. The prison's industries included a coal mine, brickyard, twine plant, and tinker shop. The tinker shop made inlaid furniture, brooms, chewing tobacco, walking sticks, pin cushions, and harnesses. Most of the work was done by hand. The profits went to the prison fund. The inmates were paid a small sum, which they used for personal items or sent to their families.

In 1956, Robert Steele, officer in charge of the rock crusher at the prison, reported production numbers for the *Twentieth Biennial Report of the Board of Penal Institutions*. Included were 11,220,000 pounds of chat (waste rock from mining), 2,358,000 pounds of concrete rock, 1,256,000 pounds of 1.5-inch rock, 2,239 loads of shale, and 1,833 loads of dirt.

The KSP twine plant began taking sisal orders in April 1900. Within 10 days, the plant shipped one-tenth of its total output (100,000 pounds) to farmers who had mail-ordered between 100 and 500 pounds of twine to use during the harvest season. The twine was made from sisal fibers imported from Mexico. The fiber is coarse and inflexible, which makes it ideal for baling hay. The twine plant was big business for the prison. In 1903, warden E.B. Jewett answered questions in front of the Kansas House of Representatives in regard to the operations of the twine plant. He stated that, in 1902, the twine plant manufactured 1,101,660 pounds of twine. George A. Myers served as plant superintendent, with Richard Eagle as assistant superintendent. Two guards served as lookouts, and 60–75 inmates worked at the plant.

In 1916, J.L. Cline, superintendent of the KSP twine plant, reported that the plant had undergone a banner year, producing 3,093,600 pounds of twine in 305 days. In response to having to stockpile sisal because of the unrest caused by the Mexican Revolution, he suggested building a 46-by-400-foot warehouse to accommodate the growing industry. He also noted that the inmates took "great pride in their work."

A group of men pose for a photograph in front of the superintendent's office at the Kansas State Penitentiary coal mine. The superintendent had to make sure that ventilation equipment and water pumps were in good working order to help ensure the safety of the officers and inmates in the mine. On occasion, accidents did happen, such as a gas explosion in December 1929 that mortally wounded two inmate miners.

John Higgins and 13 other officials pause for a photograph on mine cars. Former deputy warden Kyle Deere's great-grandfather James Liggett served as an officer down in the coal mine until a coal car struck him. Liggett lost his leg in the accident. The mine provided coal for state institutions and local schools.

The Kansas State Penitentiary used this steam shovel to assist in excavating at the facility. The officer on the far left is Joseph Waters, seen here about 1928–1930. In 1890, Kansas ranked third in coal production in the country. During the height of coal production, almost 500 inmates worked in the mine. The mine closed in 1947 due to high costs and low demand.

In the January 24, 1934, edition of the *Leavenworth Times*, Kansas State Penitentiary warden Lacey M. Simpson reported that the inmates working in the coal mine had reached an all-time record of 2,709 tons of coal mined in a week. The previous record was 1,775 tons of coal. Miners descended 720 feet into the mine, where the average vein was only 22–24 inches wide. Besides cramped quarters, inmates had to remove large amounts of shale to access the valuable coal. Inmates who worked in the mine received "good time allowed" and were paid for exceeding their quota.

Francis "Frank" Young worked at the Carr coal mine for four years before being hired on at the penitentiary coal mine as a hoisting engineer. Young was responsible for raising and lowering officers and inmates in the shaft. When the coal mine closed in 1947, Young moved to the prison machine shop, where the hardware for the gallows was made, among other things. Young worked at the prison from 1910 to 1953. (Courtesy of Eugene Young.)

Young enjoys a laugh with two of his sons Arthur (left) and Thomas (right) in the hoisting room at the penitentiary. This photograph was taken about 1942. Thomas Young was inducted into the Army at Fort Leavenworth on March 8, 1943. On October 3, 1944, he was killed by artillery fire during the battle of Forêt de Parroy, near Luneville, France. (Courtesy of Eugene Young.)

On September 16, 1897, the *Lansing News* reported a serious accident at the Kansas State Penitentiary mine. John Flint, the hoisting engineer, mistakenly turned on the steam instead of slowing the cage's descent. Carrying a dozen men, the cage fell 100 feet to the bottom of the shaft. Eight men were hospitalized at the prison for broken legs, injured ankles, and internal injuries.

In 1927, an inmate had to mine a quota of about 10 tons to earn his keep at the prison. For every ton the inmate mined above quota, he earned $1.50. Inmate Oscar Riley used his earnings to buy his mother a home in Coffeyville, Kansas. Riley had earned up to $100 for a month's work. To work in the mine, an inmate had to pass a physical examination.

The Kansas State Penitentiary coal mine was the scene of at least four mine mutinies. In 1901, 356 inmates rebelled and overpowered 18 guards in the mine. In a daring rescue, William Duckett led seven men down into the mine. A fight ensued that left five inmates dead and 25 inmates wounded. On June 26, 1927, a 77-hour mutiny ended after "loyalist" inmates overpowered the mutinous inmates. The mutiny occurred when 328 inmates took 14 officers hostage and demanded cigarettes. During the mutiny, 310 inmates in the B Cell House rioted and planned to set fire to the twine plant—a signal to the mine inmates to join them in an escape. Deputy warden R.H. Hudspeth and officers armed with sawed-off shotguns foiled the plan.

These "breaker boys" stand at the picking table in the Kansas State Penitentiary coal mine in the early 1900s. The mined coal was dumped onto the conveyor belt from the right, and the inmates sorted out the slate, rocks, and dirt before the coal went to the screens to be graded. The carbide can in the foreground contained the fuel for the miner's headlamps.

Trains posed a danger to both people and animals. On September 16, 1897, the *Lansing News* reported that a group of boys had been "hopping trains," and Howard Wilson, son of Officer Wilson, had gotten his right foot crushed by a train wheel. Then, on November 18, 1897, the *Lansing News* reported that a train had struck a horse belonging to Mr. Dust, a KSP inmate, while trying to cross the bridge.

The Kansas State Penitentiary had its own brick-making facility with large kilns to fire the bricks—about 12,000 at a time. On November 12, 1922, the *Topeka Daily Capital* reported that the legislature had made an appropriation of $65,000 to construct permanent buildings at the Kansas State Industrial Farm for Women. The dormitories were built with inmate labor and bricks made at the prison.

A mine cave-in damaged this brickyard building at the Kansas State Penitentiary. Today, core samples are taken in certain areas of Lansing before constructing new buildings to ensure there are no old coal mine tunnels that could cave in and damage a building. In 1927, the *Leavenworth Times* reported that the mine had 21 miles of tunnels.

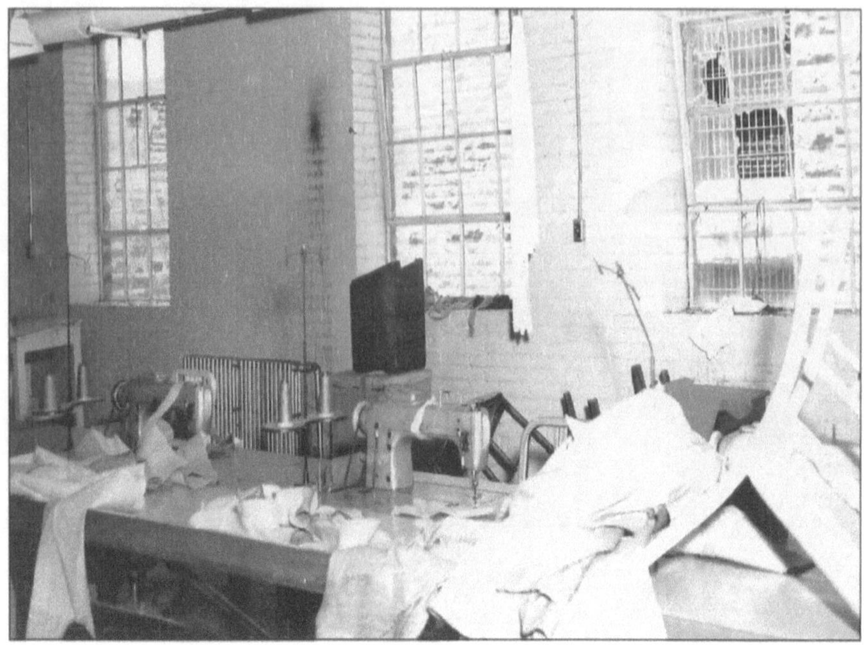

The tailor shop was located above the laundry at the prison. Inmates made officer uniforms and other items, including baseball bases, tea towels, belts, caps, hospital gowns, jumpers, baker's mittens, sheets, hospital slippers, undergarments, and aprons. The inmates in the tailor shop also repaired shoes and made clothes that were sold to other state institutions. In 1956, R. Benton, officer in charge of the tailor shop, reported $24,764.78 in sales to other state institutions for fiscal years 1954 and 1955. These photographs were taken in the aftermath of the riot on June 18, 1969. Until 2011, protective-custody inmates hemmed and repaired inmate uniforms. Today, Impact Design, a private company with a factory on the prison grounds, employs inmates to embroider logos onto clothing. The company also has a screen print and warehouse operation.

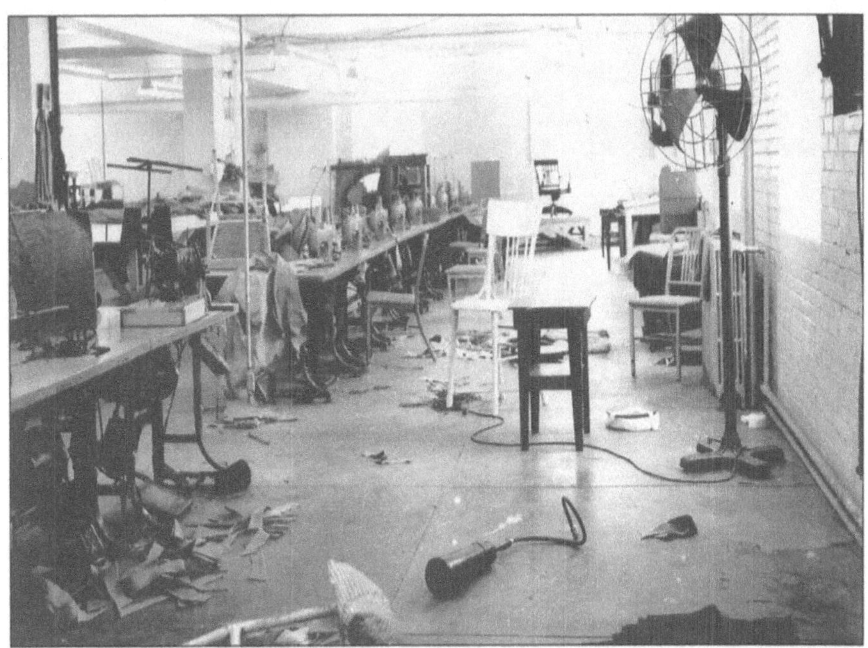

The Atchison, Topeka, and Santa Fe Railroad built a spur directly to the Kansas State Penitentiary, enabling shipment of incoming operational supplies and outgoing items produced by the prison's industries. The spur is gone, but the history of the Atchison, Topeka, and Santa Fe Railroad lives on at the Lansing Historical Museum on prison grounds.

The Kansas State Penitentiary is seen bustling with industrial activity. It is difficult to determine what the inmates are loading onto the train for shipment; possibilities include bricks made at the prison or cords of wood harvested at the prison farm. Officers in the two towers at right had a bird's-eye view of the activity.

On July 30, 1969, an arson fire caused major damage to the sign factory at the prison. Today, the metals division makes most of the signs for the Kansas Department of Transportation, as well as traffic signs and neighborhood watch signs. They also fabricate metal fire rings, kiosk stands, bike racks, detention furniture, and other products. Approximately 30 inmates work in the division.

In 1969, the Kansas State Penitentiary paint factory sustained heavy damage from an arson fire. Today, the prison continues to manufacture paint, which is used by the State of Kansas and other institutions, such as school districts. The factory annually produces 300,000 gallons of traffic paint and approximately 60,000 gallons of architectural paint. The prison also makes cleaning chemicals.

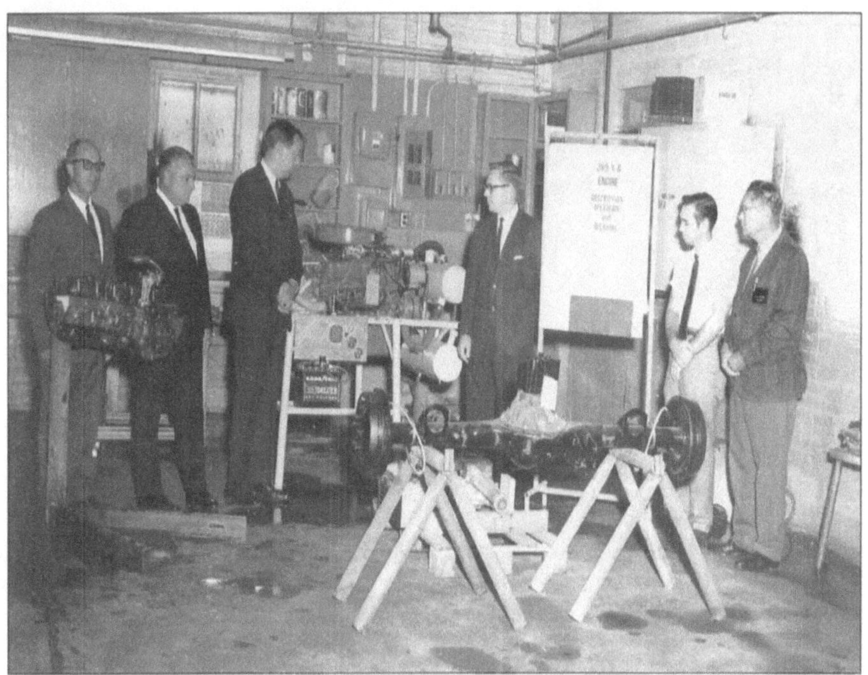

In the spring of 1970, a class of 15 Kansas State Penitentiary inmates began an automobile mechanics course. The federal Manpower Development Training program funded the 25-week course, instructed by William J. Prince of Lawrence, Kansas, and the Ford Motor Company donated a truck to the program. The inmates had to disassemble the truck to get it inside the old prison tailor shop above the laundry, where the class was being taught. Upon completion of the course, J.V. Leonhard, vocational coordinator at the prison, said the State Employment Security Division would assist inmates in finding jobs as automobile mechanics.

Inmates have participated in construction projects at LCF and throughout the community. The projects give inmates an opportunity to learn work skills that can assist them in getting a job upon release. It is also a way for the inmates to give back to the community. Using inmate labor provides financial savings as well. In the summer of 1996, an inmate work crew poured 4,330 feet of sidewalk for the city of Lansing.

A Lansing Correctional Facility inmate keeps an eye on the dozens of embroidery machines humming away in the factory. Impact Design is a private industry located within the prison. As of February 2014, Impact Design employed 247 inmates. The company embroiders and screen prints apparel for a variety of clients, including colleges and professional sports teams. (Courtesy of Phil White, LCF.)

Four

LIFE BEHIND THE WALLS

In many ways, the Lansing Correctional Facility is like a small Kansas town. With approximately 2,400 inmates and over 1,000 regular and contract staff, the population of the facility is greater than a large percentage of Kansas towns. The facility has most of the things a town would have, such as housing, industries, a health clinic, recreation areas, and so on. A less desirable aspect of prison life, just like outside the walls, is crime.

The prison has seen its fair share of violence from coal mine mutinies, assaults, murders, and incidents such as the riot on June 18, 1969. In addition to prison reform in the 1970s, correctional officers' constant vigilance for contraband items, including weapons, narcotics, and cell phones, has reduced the number of disruptions at the facility. Inmates who abide by the rules are rewarded with good behavior incentives, such as the opportunity to purchase their own television, radio, typewriter, lamp, fans, and alarm clock. In addition, inmates have the possibility of earning good time toward their eventual release. Another incentive for good behavior is musical concerts like the one County Road 5, a rock/country group, gave in January 2014.

Perhaps the most famous musician to visit the prison was Johnny Cash and his wife, June, in May 1970. Before performing at the men's prison, the couple took their infant son, John Carter Cash, to the women's prison so June could nurse her son and have lunch. Accompanied by 30 singers and musicians, Cash sang country and jailhouse songs in his signature black suit and boots. After the hour-long performance, Cash shook hands with the inmates before the group left to perform at the United States Penitentiary Leavenworth.

In the early days of the penitentiary, inmates were kept on the silent system. They were not allowed to talk to each other unless it was work related. In the late 1800s, when John Reynolds was brought to the prison, he was issued tickets that granted privileges such as tobacco, visitation rights, writing a monthly letter to family, and one book a week from the library.

A typical day for an inmate starts with breakfast at 5:30 a.m. Work call is 7:30 a.m., and the dining hall begins to serve lunch at 10:30 a.m. After an afternoon count of the inmates, dinner is served at 3:30 p.m., with evening activities starting at 6:00 p.m. The amount of yard time an inmate gets depends on work detail and good behavior.

Pictured here prior to 1907 is a Tom Thumb wedding at the Christian church within the Kansas State Penitentiary. Among those pictured are John Hardman, Esther Meriam, Ted Bird, Maud Campbell, Elsie Scott, Dorcas Hannon, Nellie Blossom, Edith Humphrey, F. Beemer, Gladys Paisl, Luther Shirley, Jimmie Yates, Carl Fulton, Ralph McBrian, Gladys Estep, Roland Estep, Laura Meriam, and Homer Walkerausher.

Dogs have been a part of life at the Kansas State Penitentiary for decades. The man offering a treat to the dog is possibly warden Kirk Prather. In addition to the K-9 Unit, the Safe Harbor Prison Dog adoption program rescues dogs in danger of euthanasia across the Midwest. The dogs live with inmate handlers and learn basic commands to prepare them for adoption. The inmates benefit from having to care for a living being and receiving unconditional affection from the dogs.

The Kansas State Penitentiary baseball team, the Red Sox, is pictured in 1928 with KSP records clerk Clyde Wilson (far left). Community ball teams went behind the walls to play the inmates. Eugene Young recalled, "In the mid- to late 1950s, our softball team went into the state prison on Saturday mornings to play a game against the inmate team. When we played the game, the inmates always rooted for our team and would run down their own team. It was great fun for us."

KSP records clerk Clyde Wilson (second from left) watches boxer Jack Johnson (left) during a match at Lansing. Johnson was serving time at the US penitentiary in Leavenworth for violating the Mann Act, which protected against the transport of women across state lines for immoral purposes. The charges stemmed from his white girlfriend Lucille Cameron's allegedly being a prostitute and because Johnson was African American. He was released on July 9, 1921.

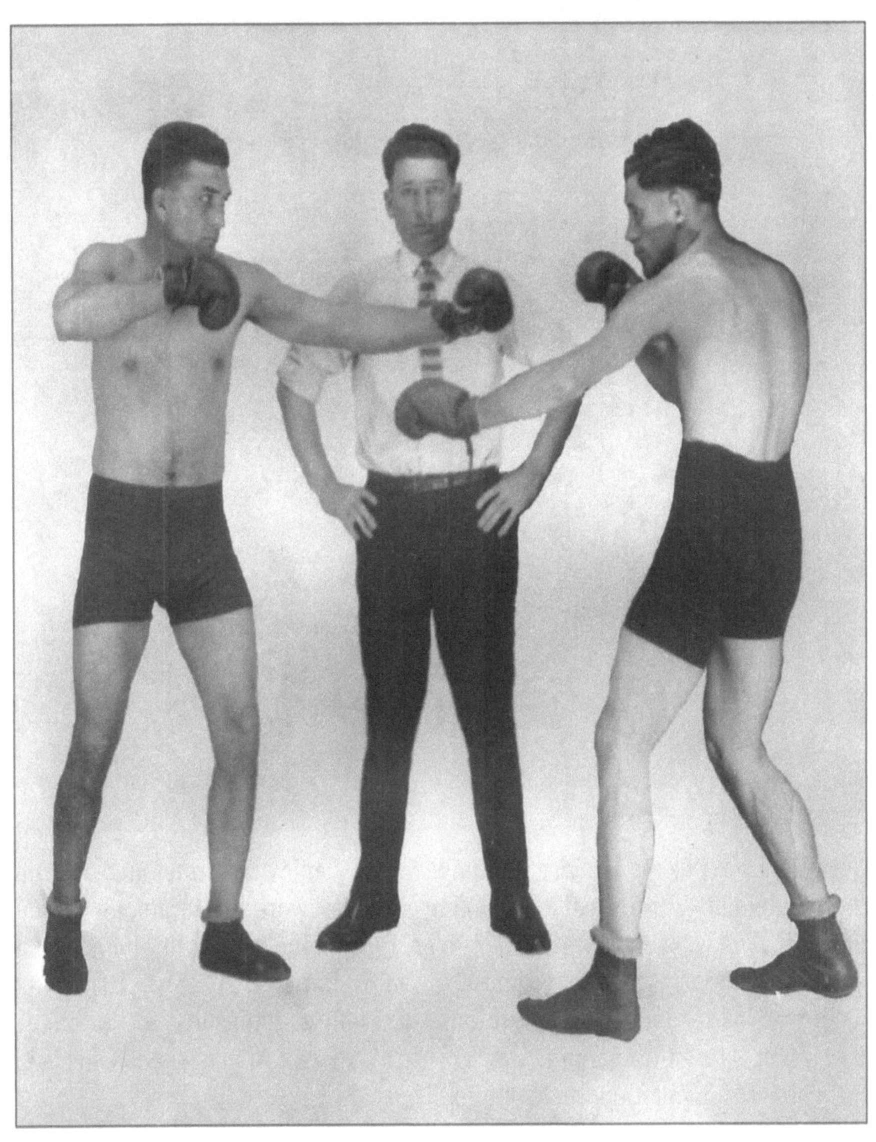

On April 26, 1928, warden W.H. Mackey announced a wrestling and boxing exhibition at 2:00 p.m. that Saturday. These exhibitions provided entertainment for both the inmates and the community. Seven boxing bouts between inmates across different weight classes were scheduled for three to five rounds. Today, LCF offers basketball, baseball, volleyball, soccer, handball, racquetball, and non-contact football. Community teams compete against the inmate basketball and baseball teams.

Seen here next to the laundry building, inmates enjoy watermelon grown on the penitentiary farm. In the beginning, inmates wore the infamous striped uniform. Today, inmate attire consists of a light blue shirt with blue jeans, a navy belt, boots, and a red baseball cap. Inmates are also issued an identification badge. The exceptions are yellow jumpsuits for privilege restriction, brown for segregation, green for Special Management Unit, and light blue for orientation/transportation.

The man in this image is believed to be Kirk Prather, who served as a warden at the Kansas State Penitentiary in the 1930s. He is holding two shotguns, with a Savidge 99 rifle on the table. Inmates took Prather and other officers hostage during a Memorial Day baseball game. One of the inmate bank robbers in the escape ensured the hostages' safety and freed them when the group reached Oklahoma.

This c. 1928 photograph shows an inmate trusty in downtown Lansing, along with a little boy, his dog, and a business owner. While this type of trusty program no longer exists, the Lansing Correctional Facility does have inmate work crews that provide assistance in the area. When a tornado hit Tonganoxie, Kansas, on May 11, 2000, an LCF work crew was on scene within an hour, clearing debris from the storm.

Members of the Nine Mile 4-H Club pose in front of the Kansas State Penitentiary. From left to right are (first row) Bob Wilcox, Bob Younghans, Ben Lohman, Victor Parisa, and Ben Wilcox; (second row) unidentified, Maxine Lohman, Rosemary Parisa, unidentified, and Marie Gaiger; (third row) Bob Davis, ? Wilcox, three unidentified, and Hulda Parisa. Creeks and the like in the area were named in relation to how far they were from Fort Leavenworth, hence the name *Nine Mile*.

Here is another photograph of the Nine Mile 4-H Club. From left to right are (first row) Russell Edmonds, Bernice Edmonds, Chester Edmonds, Charles Edmonds, Howard Edmonds, Victor Parisa, Mike Amrine, Abbie Amrine, and Rosemary Parisa; (second row) Orville Edmonds, Glenn Linaweaver, Bessie Gaiser, Winnie Wilcox, and Minnie Wilcox; (third row) Margaret Lineaweaver, Mrs. Jacob Gaiser, Pearl Edmonds, Mrs. Amrine, Iva Holliday, Louise Jamison, Ruth Wilcox, Dorothy Jamison, and Marie Gaiser; (fourth row) Matt Edmonds, warden M.F. Amrine, Hulda Parisa, Claude Lineaweaver, and May Wilcox.

Siblings J.T. and Grace Brown pose for an inmate photographer. Their grandfather, Jesse Crouch, worked at the prison. The Lansing Historical Museum has approximately two dozen glass-plate negatives of male and female mug shots from the early 1900s. For decades, 35mm film was used to photograph the world. Today, the Lansing Correctional Facility uses digital cameras to document inmates and prison life.

Warden M.F. Amrine is pictured with his wife and children, from left to right, Abbie, Mike, Dorothy, and Mary. Mike Amrine became an author, co-writing articles with scientists Harold Urey and Albert Einstein. He also was instrumental in passing the legislation that created the Atomic Energy Commission. At the time of his death in 1974, Mike Amrine was assistant to Dr. Theodore Cooper, director of the National Heart and Lung Institute.

In June 1969, approximately 130 Kansas State Highway Patrol troopers from across the state responded to the riot call to restore order at the Kansas State Penitentiary. Gail Banker Armstrong, daughter of J.J. Banker, lived in one of the officer houses on Kansas Avenue. According to Armstrong, law enforcement officers had set up a perimeter around the prison, and she had to have a police escort to get back to her house. Due to a shortage of correctional officers, a smaller force of troopers stayed to keep watch from the towers until late October 1969.

Inmates from the A Cell House clean up after the riot at the Kansas State Penitentiary on June 18, 1969. During the riot, inmates broke windows, tore out catwalk railings, set small fires, and badly damaged the locking systems in the A and C Cell Houses. The total loss to the facility was valued at a quarter million dollars. In today's currency, it would be approximately $1.57 million.

After the 1969 riot, 182 men were housed in a compound inside the prison, consisting of mobile buildings and tents surrounded by a chain-link fence and armed officers. The prison reintegrated inmates back into the main prison population, and by July 9, only 46 inmates remained in the temporary compound. To protest their living conditions, the remaining inmates set fire to the mobile buildings in the compound.

Correctional officers are constantly on the lookout for contraband weapons. Two slang terms often heard in popular culture are "shank" and "shiv," which are often used interchangeably. More specifically, a shiv is a sharply pointed object, and a shank is a knife-like weapon. Mundane items such as spoons and pieces of Plexiglas can be shaped into a weapon. Possessing, selling, distributing, or soliciting dangerous contraband is a Class 1 offense. The penalty may combine any or all of the following: disciplinary segregation, loss of "good time credits," extra work, solitary confinement, restriction from privileges, fines, restitution, and an oral or written reprimand.

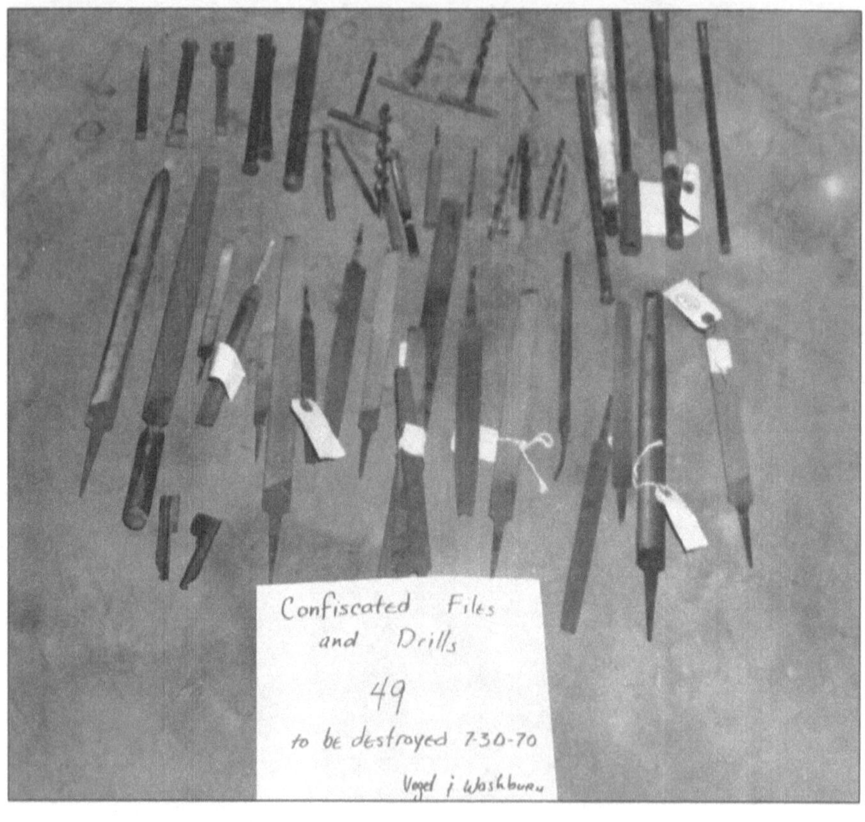

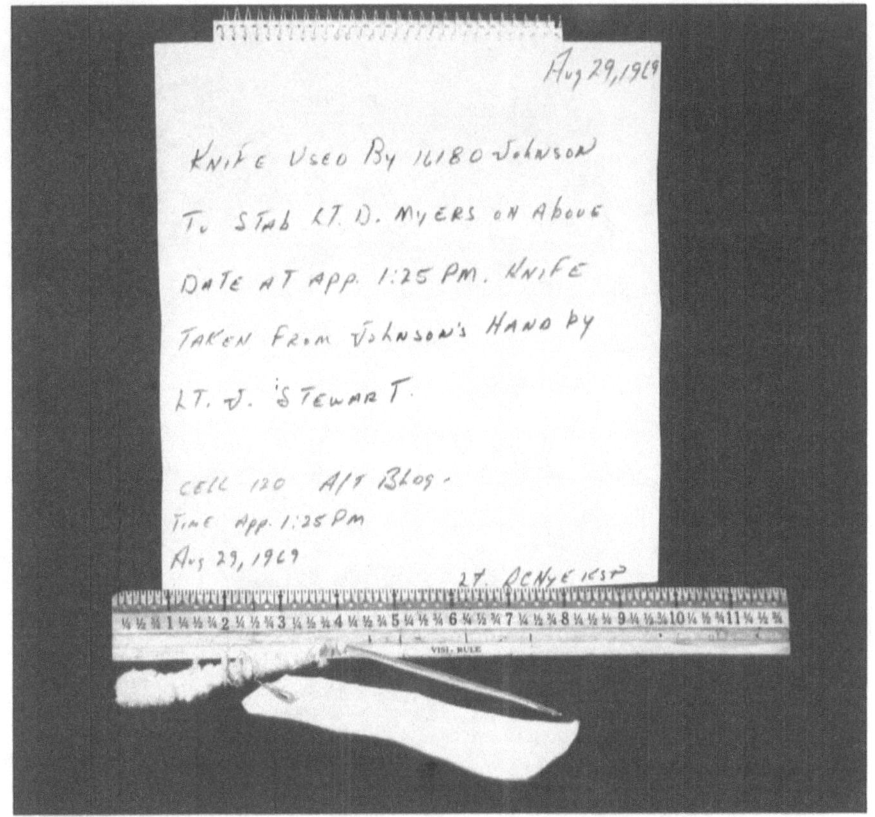

Lansing Correctional Facility officers often deal with dangerous situations in the prison. On August 29, 1969, inmate Johnson, No. 16180, used the handmade knife above to stab Lt. D. Myers at about 1:25 p.m. Lt. J. Stewart confiscated the weapon at the Adjustment and Treatment Building. On April 24, 1972, Lieutenant Dunkley and Officer Miller discovered a piece of saw blade and other weapons in Johnson's shoes in the East Wing of the Adjustment and Treatment Building. Another instance of violence against staff occurred on August 15, 1969, when an inmate seriously injured officer Travis J. Adams by throwing bricks and pieces of cement at him. In April 1970, the inmate pleaded guilty to "maiming, wounding, and doing great bodily harm."

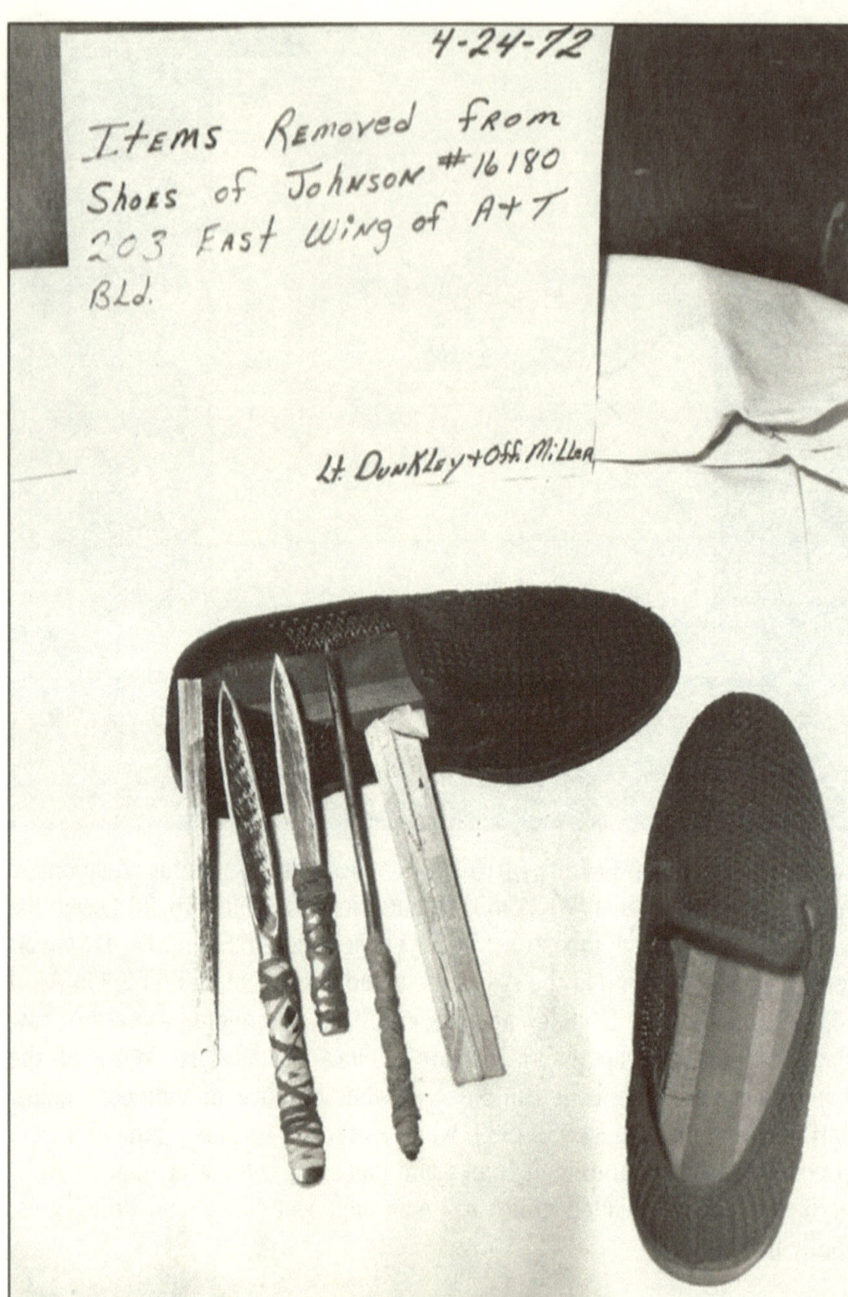

4-24-72
Items Removed from
Shoes of Johnson # 16180
203 East Wing of A+T
Bld.
Lt. Dunkley + Off. Miller

Lansing Correctional Facility officers are always on the lookout for narcotics contraband. In this 1970 seizure, officers confiscated 13.5 pounds of marijuana, 0.75 pound of nutmeg, 1.125 pounds of chicken powder, 15.25 pounds of pills, 213 Wyamine (misspelled here as "Wymire," a mild stimulant that could cause hallucinations if abused), 750 needles, and 195 syringes. Nutmeg may appear to be benign; however, consuming large quantities of the spice will cause hallucinations. Needles are even more of a concern to staff due to the possibility of transmission of blood-borne pathogens such as the hepatitis B virus, hepatitis C, and human immunodeficiency virus (HIV). (Courtesy of Gail Banker Armstrong.)

On July 30, 1969, two Leavenworth fire trucks and two Delaware Township Volunteer Fire Department trucks raced to the Kansas State Penitentiary to fight a fire in the highway marker plant in the northeast corner of the prison. The fire was discovered at 3:30 p.m., shortly after inmates assigned to the sign plant had left work and returned to their cells. The fire did $35,000 in damage, which would be $226,367 today. The firefighters were repeatedly called to the prison that year to battle arson fires that caused extensive damage to industrial buildings and the education department building.

On October 4, 1969, fire trucks from Leavenworth and Delaware Townships responded to a fire in the food cannery underneath a dining hall. Approximately 15 firefighters, along with prison staff and inmates, fought the fire. Leavenworth fire chief Ed Zobel described it as a "really stubborn blaze." The firefighters had to break through a cinder-block wall to get to the fire. The arson fire did $11,052 in damages.

Prior to the 1969 fire in the cannery, inmates were canning tomatoes and making ketchup. The fire disrupted the production, and as a result, part of the penitentiary's tomato crop spoiled. Arson was suspected since the door leading to the cannery had been pried open. The prison placed some inmates in close custody for further questioning about the fire, which was investigated by prison officials and a deputy state fire marshal.

Dr. Robert Moore served as a physician for the Kansas State Penitentiary and the surrounding community. He objected to capital punishment and yet did his duty to legally declare the deaths of executed inmates. A veteran of both World Wars, Moore was also active in the Saddle Club and served on the Lansing school board.

Warden Sherman Crouse and his wife, Bonnie, are pictured at his retirement party. Crouse served as warden from 1963 to 1970, during which time he dealt with difficult situations. On April 14, 1965, KSP executed Perry Smith and Richard Hickock. On June 22, 1965, George York and James Latham were the last inmates to be executed in Kansas. In the summer of 1969, unrest broke out with a riot and subsequent acts of arson and violence.

KSP staff members receive certificates after completing a motivational training seminar in 1971 or 1972. From left to right are (first row) director Robert Woodson, deputy warden J.J. Banker, six unidentified, parole officer Larry Wheeler, counselor Sam Jones, warden R.J. Gaffney, and training officer Dallas Wetzel; (second row) unidentified, officer William Randolf, officer Keller, unidentified, and penal clerk John Cooling. The rest are unidentified.

In addition to being captain, R.F. Earls was in charge of security at the
Kansas State Penitentiary in 1966. He later became deputy warden of

programs, and upon the death of deputy warden J.J. Banker, Earls became deputy warden of security. John Cooling, who worked at the prison from May 9, 1966, to April 1, 2007, said Earls was well liked and stood up for the officers and other prison personnel.

From left to right are Kansas State Penitentiary deputy warden J.J. Banker, Kansas state representative James C. Ford, and Virgie Banker. Prior to becoming deputy warden, J.J. Banker served as information officer for the penitentiary. Representative Ford, a Democrat farmer from Stevens County, served District 122 in the Kansas House of Representatives. Virgie Banker, wife of deputy warden Banker, was a senior officer at the women's prison in Lansing. (Courtesy of Gail Banker Armstrong.)

Kansas State Penitentiary captain Dallas Wetzel and inmate clerk Eddie Cox pose for a photograph. A retired Army sergeant, Wetzel had different positions at the prison during his tenure, including training officer, acting major, and head of outside work details.

Warden R.J. Gaffney (center) retired from the US Disciplinary Barracks and came to Lansing in 1970, serving until 1973. According to Eugene Young, Gaffney "wasn't afraid of a darn thing." Describing Gaffney as hands-on, Ed Simons said Gaffney, alone, walked right inside to talk to the inmates during a sit-in. Also under Gaffney, small televisions were allowed inside cells for the first time to reward inmates for good behavior.

The prison has always attracted former members of the military as a new career path. From left to right are the following retired military men: Lt. Col. Bob Bachtel (Marines), industries accounting II; S.Sgt. Dallas Wetzel (Army), training; Chief Warrant Officer Robert Murotake (Army), social worker; Col. George Clark (Army), industries supervisor; 1st Sgt. R.F. Earls (Air Force), deputy warden MT; Chief Warrant Officer Sterling Allen (Army), training; Lt. Comdr. C.H. Wheatley (Navy), industries production manager; Lt. Col. R.J. Gaffney (Army), warden (seated); S.Sgt. R.V. Oliver (Army), class and records; Chief Warrant Officer William Barker (Army), records; Maj. Richard Alspaugh, (Army), inmate classification; S.Sgt. Charles Johnson (Army), director of security; Lt. Col. Robert Van Horn (Army), director of education; and Col. Robert Atkins (Army), consultant.

Pictured at this table in the maximum-security kitchen are, from left to right, Ed Simons, chaplain; R.J. Gaffney, warden; George Conklin, recreation director; J.J Banker, deputy warden; unidentified; James Post, chaplain; and unidentified. During the 99th Congress of Corrections in Minnesota, Post received the Chaplain of the Year award for his service as an Army chaplain during World War II. After coming to KSP in 1956, he organized the prison choir and sponsored the KSP chapter of Alcoholics Anonymous.

On July 1, 1962, Miriam Phillips became superintendent of the Kansas State Industrial Farm for Women. She had been the head group supervisor at the Los Guilucos School for Girls in California. In 1968, Phillips Hall was dedicated in her honor. Today, Phillips Hall serves as the visiting room of East Unit, along with a gymnasium for activities. The faith-based group Brothers in Blue Reentry uses the facility for their programming as well.

Inmates can enroll in the GED program provided by Greenbush. According to one inmate, "It's a stepping stone to where I want to get." Donnelly College offers minimum- and medium-security inmates the opportunity to take freshman and sophomore college classes leading to an associate of arts degree. Of the 208 students who have been released, only eight have suffered from recidivism or violated their parole.

On October 20, 1969, the penitentiary began a sales training course for inmates under the federal Manpower Development Training Act. J.V. Leonhard detailed the course curriculum with the following subjects: salesmanship, warehousing, merchandising, interior store display, buying, invoicing, and market merchandise. Upon release, the inmates would receive job placement assistance. If the position required bonding, the federal government would bond the inmate for up to $10,000 a year. (Courtesy of Gail Banker Armstrong.)

Dr. Karl Menninger was a national leader in the field of psychiatry. In 1971, he visited the prison as an advisor to Gov. Robert Docking. One of the positive changes he noted in the prison was the introduction of television. Today, televisions are allowed inside the cells. To prevent inmates from hiding contraband, the televisions have a special seal as well as a clear window to see inside the device.

Music plays an important role in rehabilitation. Over the years, musicians such as Charlie Horton and his Western Band (pictured), Johnny Cash, and County Road 5 have performed at the prison. A personal friend of warden R.J. Gaffney, Horton played a 90-minute show on the prison baseball diamond in 1970. Concerts are a way to reward good behavior among the inmates.

On August 6–9, 1970, the Kansas State Penitentiary held its first annual arts and crafts show at the Leavenworth Plaza. The show featured leather goods, loom-woven place mats, oil and pastel paintings, tablecloths, furniture covers, hand-woven rugs, working matchstick models of automobiles, stagecoaches, and other items. Proceeds went to the inmates, the majority of whom sent the funds home to family. (Courtesy of Gail Banker Armstrong.)

Art has long been used as part of the rehabilitation process. For years, Arts in Prison Inc., a nonprofit organization in Overland Park, Kansas, has provided music, writing, gardening, yoga, and visual and performing arts programs at the Lansing Correctional Facility. Studies have shown that inmates who participate in art programs have a lower recidivism rate than those who do not participate.

Kansas State Penitentiary activities director George Conklin (left) and warden R.J. Gaffney (right) are pictured with the Red Sox inmate baseball team. On August 27, 1970, the *Leavenworth Times* reported that pitcher Steve Kline, left-handed hitter Pete Ward, pitcher Ron Klimkowski, and pitcher Gary Waslewski of the New York Yankees conducted a baseball clinic for the inmates. Red Sox left-handed pitcher Sherm Coleman struck out Ward during the exhibition. (Courtesy of Gail Banker Armstrong.)

At five foot five and 146 pounds, Kansas State Penitentiary inmate Donald Blue (center) set a national record in the dead lift of 600 pounds. Besides winning weight-lifting awards, Blue was a strong supporter of the women's liberation movement and distributed pamphlets about women's physical fitness to high schools and colleges. (Courtesy of Gail Banker Armstrong.)

This group of Kansas State Penitentiary officers posed for a photograph as they were promoted from correctional officers I to correctional officers II, which gave them more supervisor responsibility. In the second row, third and fourth from left, are Howell Alligood and Major Johnson. Today, Howell Alligood's son Mark is a firefighter and emergency medical technician at Leavenworth County Fire District No. 1, located on the prison grounds. (Courtesy of Gail Banker Armstorng.)

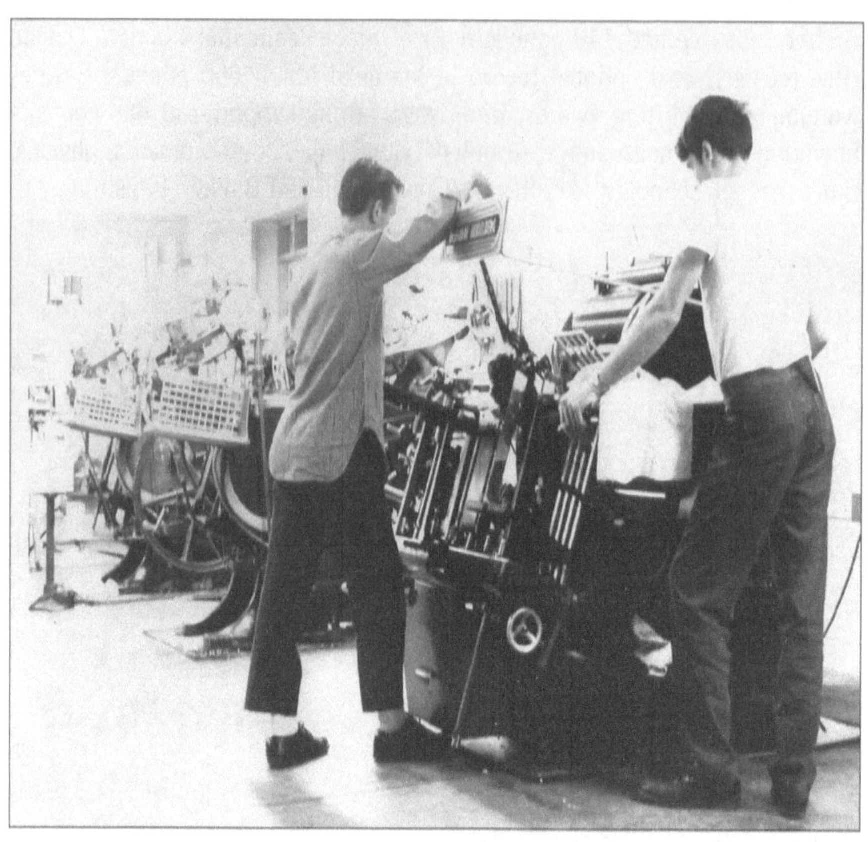

Two Kansas State Penitentiary inmates operate a printing press. In 1916, chaplain Harmon Allen reported that the prison newspaper, the *Penitentiary Bulletin*, had changed its name to the *Square Deal*. It was a weekly inmate publication with a circulation of 890 inside and 610 outside the walls. The income from the publication went to the relief fund for the destitute families of inmates.

Lansing native Robert Woodson (at podium) started his law enforcement career in 1955 at the Leavenworth County Sheriff's Office. He served two terms as sheriff, from 1959 to 1962, and was appointed Leavenworth police chief in 1963. On February 20, 1967, Governor Docking appointed him as superintendent of the Kansas Highway Patrol. Docking appointed Woodson as the director of the prison system on July 1, 1969, and he served in that capacity through July 27, 1973.

Seen here is a Kansas State Penitentiary staff and family picnic at Lost 80 Park. Among those pictured are Mrs. Wetzel (left), deputy warden J.J. Banker (center), and captain Dallas Wetzel (right). Today, the city of Lansing leases Lost 80 Park from the Lansing Correctional Facility. Local lore has it that the park got its name because, for a number of years, those at the prison were unaware of the land, then rediscovered that it belonged to them.

Kansas State Penitentiary officers are seen at a training session in the administration building. At the table on the right are Francis L. Benner (front left), Richard C. Worthington (rear left), and Jacob Moppin (front right). All officers and non-officers received weapons training. Self-defense was not taught at the time.

Kansas State Penitentiary officer Jacob Moppin and his wife, Martha Moppin (center), peruse the leather goods made by the inmates in the early 1970s. Also identified is Ada Young (far right). According to the *Leavenworth Times*, thousands of people visited the first Kansas State Penitentiary arts and crafts show at Leavenworth Plaza in 1970.

Today, Leavenworth County Fire District No. 1 provides fire protection for LCF. The truck is escorted to the area where the fire is located. The inmates are generally in lockdown during a fire, and a staff member watches the truck while the firefighters extinguish the fire. Fire department investigators work alongside with LCF's investigators to determine the cause of the fire. District No. 1 also provides basic fire-safety training to officers.

Over the years, the inactive Delaware Cemetery fell into disrepair. Organizations tried to clean up the cemetery; however, sustaining the cleanup efforts proved problematic. In the autumn of 1982, inmates began to clear out the brush. Officer Riner said, "These fellows feel like they're really accomplishing something. When they get back inside and start talking about what their crew got done that day, these fellows seem to enjoy it." (Author's collection.)

Some inmates are permitted to work outside the Lansing Correctional Facility walls in a private industry to gain job experience as well as income. Currently, inmates work at Henke Manufacturing, Heatron Inc., and Zephyr Products Inc. in Leavenworth. Inmates also work at the Impact Design division in Overland Park. Henke manufactures snowplows, industrial snow equipment, hitches, and attachments. In addition to custom LED lighting solutions, Heatron builds custom heaters and heating elements. Zephyr provides metals fabrication, welding, and other related services. Impact Design creates embroidered and screen-printed apparel.

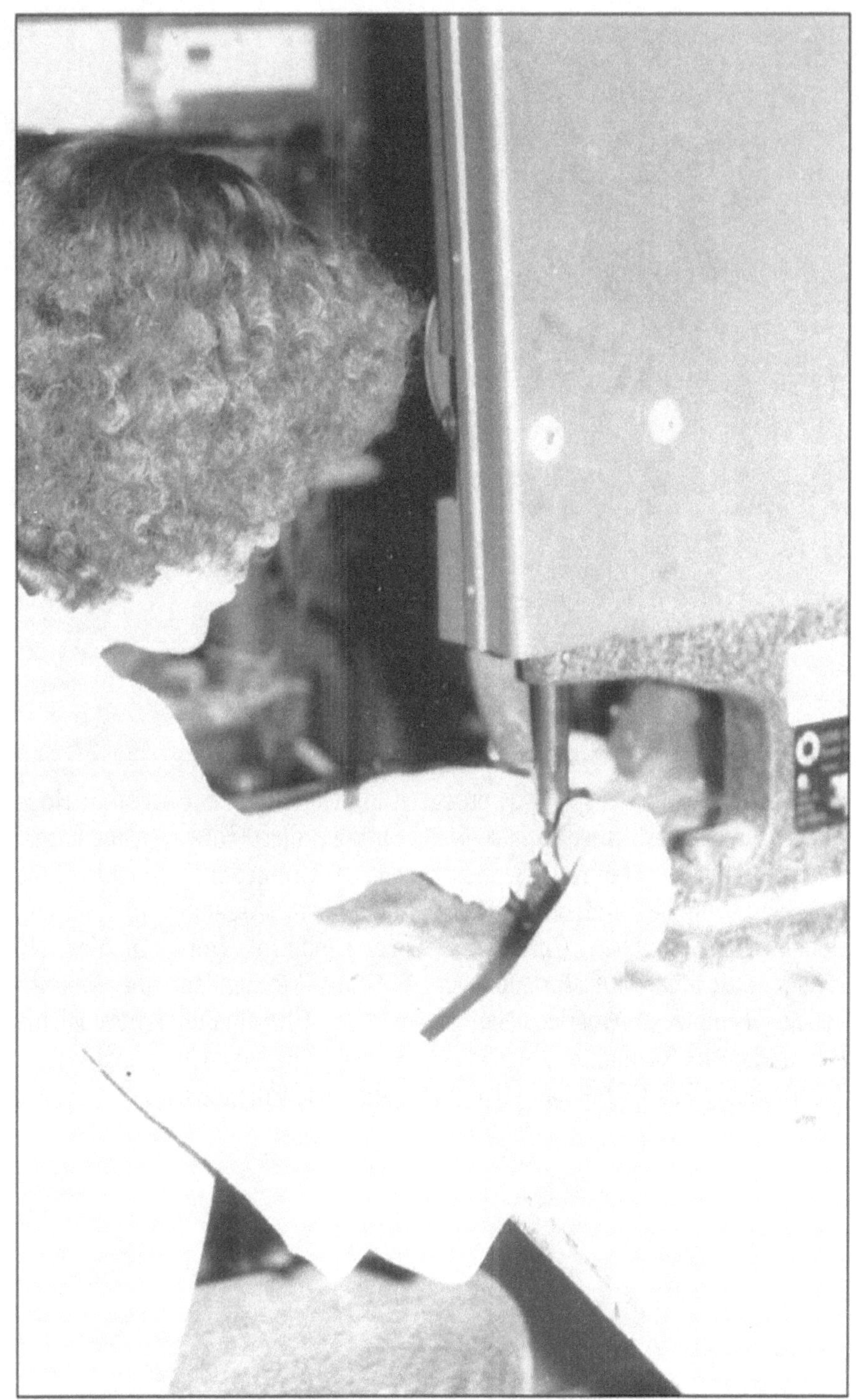

When an All Faiths Chapel was proposed in the 1970s, the Beacon of Hope Chapel Singers performed to raise funds for the project. However, the chapel was never built. The Kansas Department of Corrections recognizes the following churches and religions: Ásatrú/Odinism, Assembly of Yahweh, Buddhism, Catholicism, Christian Science, Hinduism, House of Yahweh, Islam, Jehovah's Witnesses, Judaism, Krishna, Mormonism, the Moorish Science Temple of America, Native American, Christianity, Protestantism, Rastafarianism, Seventh-day Adventist, Sikhism, Thelema, Unity, and Wicca. As of January 2014, LCF had 15 of these religious affiliations.

On August 28, 1971, the Beacon of Hope Chapel Choir singers participated in a community Mass led by Fr. Edward Simons at Lost 80 Park. During the service, the inmates sung hymns, and afterward, the inmates and community members had a picnic together. During the holidays, the inmates would ride on a trailer, which was pulled through the streets of Lansing, singing Christmas carols to residents.

Richard Dunn (left) has served as a chaplain at LCF for over seven years and is also a brigade chaplain with the Kansas Army National Guard. Chaplain Don Almond (right) has served at Lansing for 10 years, in addition to being the pastor for Trinity United Methodist Church in Leavenworth. He preaches in the minimum- and medium-security units. Both men counsel inmates and staff during times of crisis. (Courtesy of Renda Craft, LCF.)

This medicine wheel at LCF is part of the religious ceremony for some Native American inmates, one of whom wrote the following: "The representation of the buffalo skull shows one is paying respect and honor to life, wisdom, strength, and the Great Spirit, by placing it in the center facing south, shows a reverence to the 'Red Road,' which again is the cultural and spiritual balance of the Native existence." (Courtesy of Phil White, LCF.)

Beatrice "Bea" Wardlow checks an inmate for contraband. As of February 2014, the Lansing Correctional Facility had 480 correctional staff members. Of that number, 106 were women. To become a corrections officer, a candidate has to be at least 19 years old, have a driver's license, and pass the corrections officer test, employment and background checks, a physical exam, a drug test, and a tuberculosis test.

The Lansing Correctional Facility staff is multigenerational and multicultural. The officer fourth from left is part of the Special Operations and Response Team (SORT), which responds to unrest and emergencies at the prison. The team has three units: Tactical, Logistics, and Crisis Resolution. Other officers can wear a Class A uniform (fifth from left) or the black polo shirt with BDU trousers (far right). Administrative staff wears regular business attire. (Courtesy of Phil White, LCF.)

Five

FEMALE INMATES
AT LANSING

In the early days of the Kansas State Penitentiary, there were few female inmates. Those who were sent to Lansing were housed in the women's ward. Hosting male and female inmates in the same facility comes with its own set of problems. Therefore, in 1916, Kansas State Industrial Farm for Women was established on the penitentiary's farm and operated as a branch of the men's facility. In 1917, it became a separate satellite unit under the supervision of the State Board of Administration (Correctional Institutions Section), along with the Kansas State Penitentiary and Industrial Reformatory in Hutchinson. Later, the Board of Penal Institutions, the precursor to the Kansas Department of Corrections, oversaw the institution.

In the beginning, when the women were housed in tents with no locks, Julia Perry served as the first superintendent. On November 12, 1922, the *Topeka Daily Capital* published an article titled "Where Unfortunate Kansas Women Have Chance to Come Back," which discussed the new institution. The legislature had appropriated $65,000 to construct permanent buildings to house the female inmates. State architect Ray Gamble designed the brick cottages, built with inmate labor and bricks made at the Kansas State Penitentiary.

In 1980, the facility became co-correctional, and in 1983, the institution went through another name change to Kansas Correctional Institution at Lansing. For a short time, another name for the facility was Kansas Correctional Institution for Women. In 1988, the minimum- and medium-security female inmates were sent to the Topeka Correctional Facility, and the maximum-security women followed in April 1995. Currently, the facility is known as East Unit, which houses the minimum-security male inmates of the Lansing Correctional Facility.

This is an aerial view of the Kansas State Industrial Farm for Women. In 1983, the institution became known as the Kansas Correctional Institute at Lansing. In 1988, the minimum- and medium-security female inmates were transferred to the Topeka Correctional Facility. In 1995, the remaining women were transferred to Topeka. Today, the area is known as East Unit, which houses the minimum-security male inmates of the Lansing Correctional Facility.

A little-known chapter of the women's farm history is the large percentage of women and girls who were sent there for VC-205, a violation of Chapter 205, which was a 1917 quarantine law. If a woman sought treatment for a sexually transmitted disease, the doctor turned her in to the county health officer. She was then sent to Lansing for an indefinite sentence. This practice continued until 1956.

Miriam Phillips came from California with liberal views on rehabilitation. She believed in teaching "her girls" practical life and job skills. In accordance with her more lenient approach, their rooms were only locked at night. According to Ed Simons, an incident occurred where one of the inmates, who was under the influence drugs, began threatening others with scissors. The inmate was taken to St. John Hospital, where Phillips spent the night with her. Phillips wanted the woman to know someone cared about her.

On October 23, 1969, the inmates prepared a hot lunch for a group of 50 Fort Leavenworth military wives who were touring the farm. Mrs. Cataldo asked if the inmates resented the tour, but Phillips believed otherwise, as they welcomed the revenue from the small fee collected from the women. The funds were used to purchase needed equipment for the recreation program at the institution.

Superintendent Miriam Phillips (left), chaplain Ed Simons (second from left), and warden R.J. Gaffney (second from right) are pictured with other unidentified corrections officials at either a GED or cosmetology graduation for female inmates. Phillips expected corrections officials from Topeka and the Kansas State Penitentiary warden to attend these graduations, as it was important to her to recognize the girls for their achievements.

Here, Phillips poses with an inmate choir. Enrichment programs are an important part of the rehabilitation process. The Kansas State Industrial Farm for Women also had a ceramics program and an inmate newsletter that had at least two different names over the years: the *Gazette* and the *Hilltopper*. The sewing department made curtains, dresses, housecoats, and undergarments, and also mended garments. They also did artwork for their bazaar, which was held in the fall.

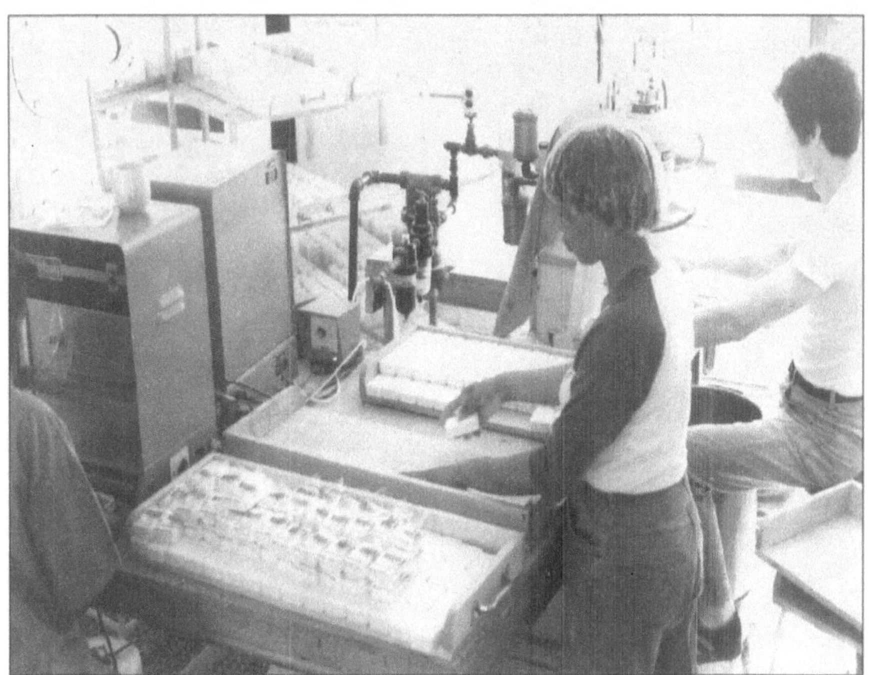

Inmates at the Kansas State Industrial Farm for Women are seen packaging bars of soap. While Kansas Correctional Industries no longer produces bars of soap, it does manufacture laundry detergent, dish soap, liquid hand soap, and professional-strength hand cleanser. Kansas Correctional Industries also manufactures janitorial cleaning supplies and products such as floor wax.

A female inmate does laundry at the Kansas State Industrial Farm for Women. Today, at the Lansing Correctional Facility, laundry for the medium- and maximum-security inmates is done in the max unit. The minimum-security inmates do their laundry at East Unit. Jeans are marked and washed together. Inmates place their socks and underwear in laundry bags to be washed.

Marie York (now Arnold) worked at the Kansas Correctional Institution at Lansing from 1984 to 1990 and retired as a first sergeant. She was in charge of the We Care for Kids program at the women's prison. In 1989 and 1990, the inmates organized a carnival picnic for low-income children from the Lansing-Leavenworth area. A drawing was held for one boy's bike and one girl's bike.

On December 5, 1987, Barbara J. Carter became the last director of the Kansas Correctional Institution at Lansing. She believed community involvement was critical to the rehabilitation of inmates. She wanted residents to think of KCIL "as part of the community, not just that place on the hill." She also wanted to expand vocational training for the women.

Six

THE FLAGSHIP OF KDOC

The Lansing Correctional Facility is considered the flagship of the Kansas Department of Corrections. In 1993, LCF became the oldest adult facility to receive a perfect score in an accreditation audit of the American Correctional Association. LCF staff are recognized for their service to corrections and the community. In addition to the staff, the facility's rehabilitation programs are highly regarded.

In November 2013, the CBS Evening News featured SuEllen Fried of Reaching Out From Within, a program that teaches inmates how to be kinder and more empathetic toward others. While the national recidivism rate is 50 percent, Kansas as a whole is about 33 percent, and inmates who regularly participate in this program have a recidivism rate of less than 10 percent. The program is so successful that it has spread to the other KDOC institutions. Other successful programs at the Lansing Correctional Facility include Arts in Prison, Brothers in Blue Reentry, and Safe Harbor Prison Dog.

Community service is important to staff and inmates alike. The facility partners with the city of Lansing and other organizations to improve the lives of those outside the walls. With an operating budget of $40,585,869 in fiscal year 2014, the Lansing Correctional Facility has had a significant economic impact on the community. For the past 146 years, the prison has stood watch over the area and been a good neighbor to the community.

The East Hill Singers, a choir composed of Lansing Correctional Facility inmates and community members, performs at area churches. Typically, the choir is composed of half inmates and half community members. Elvera Voth founded the East Hill Singers in 1996 and retired in 2008. Today, the choir is led by conductor Kirk Carson, who has been with the choir since 2006. (Courtesy of LCF.)

The East Hill Singers program is beneficial to the inmates. Not only do they gain musical training and experience, but they also learn to collaborate and respect others' talents and abilities. When asked what the program meant to him, an inmate replied, "Hope. Hope that I can do something good when I get out. Hope that I can be accepted back into society." Community singers serve as role models to the inmates. (Courtesy of LCF.)

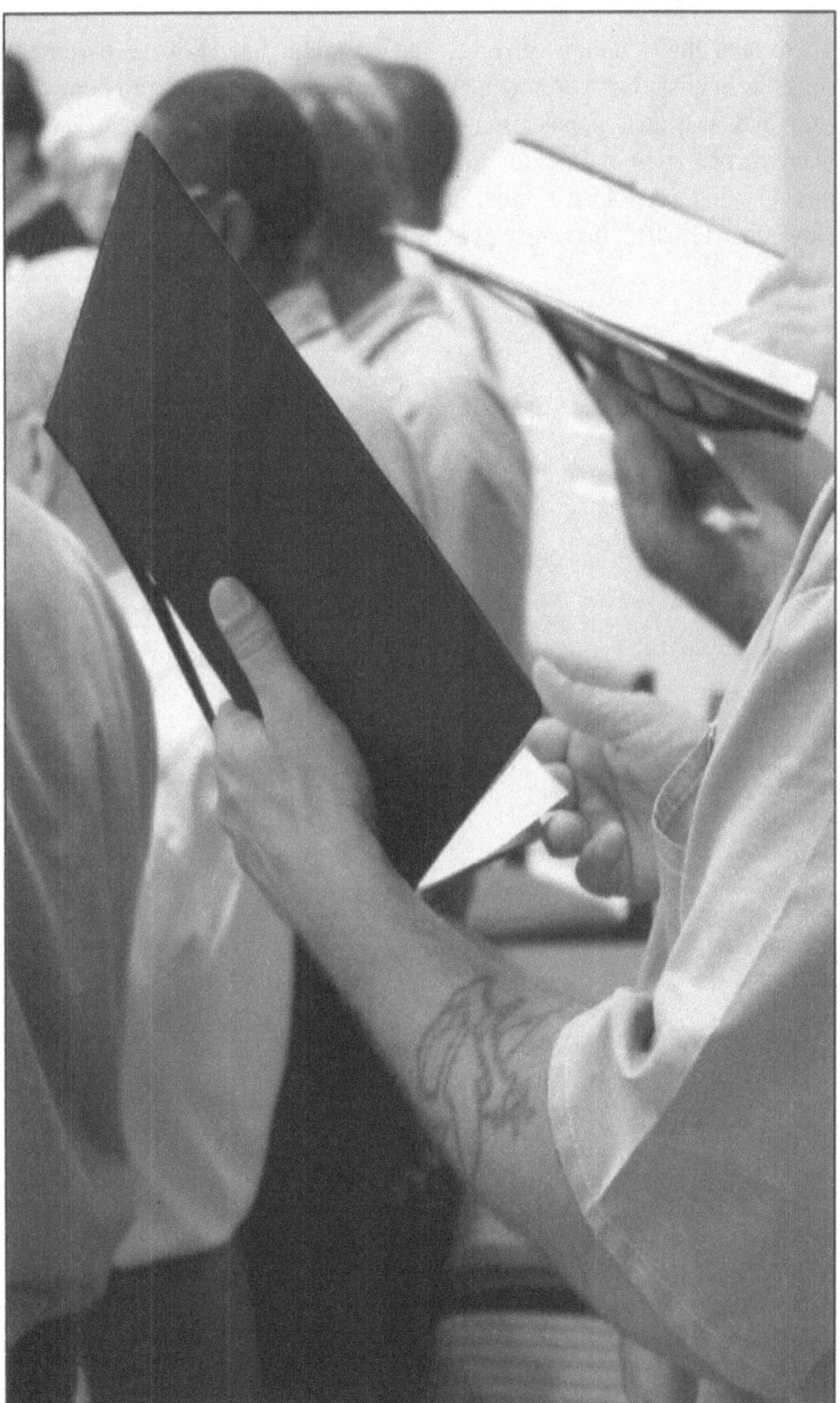

To expand their cultural offerings, the East Hill Singers have performed songs in English, Latin, Russian, Spanish, Chinese, Italian, and Hebrew. The choir has also done popular songs like "The Lion Sleeps Tonight," which many recognize from *The Lion King* soundtrack. The East Hill Singers sang this selection at the First United Methodist Church in Lawrence, Kansas, on November 11, 2012. (Courtesy of LCF.)

Grandma SuEllen Fried of Prairie Village, Kansas, visits the Lansing Correctional Facility to facilitate the Reaching Out From Within program.

Fried has been volunteering at the prison since 1977. Approximately five years later, she and an inmate serving a life sentence created the program to help break the cycle of violence that often leads people to serve time in prison. (Courtesy of SuEllen Fried.)

Sultan fell off an 18-foot embankment and broke two of his legs. The Safe Harbor Prison Dog adoption program rescued Sultan and paid his medical bills. Since August 13, 2004, Safe Harbor has taken in thousands of unwanted dogs that were to be euthanized. About 100 inmates are trained as dog handlers, spending countless hours training and socializing the dogs to prepare them for adoption to the public. (Courtesy of LCF.)

The LCF Bike Giveaway program began on a volunteer basis among inmates in 1999. The inmates in the program take used bicycles and refurbish them. At the end of the year, service groups collect the bicycles and give them to families in need. The program, which has rebuilt and distributed thousands of bicycles to area communities, allows inmates to work as a team to accomplish the goal of helping others. (Courtesy of Phil White, LCF.)

In June 2001, floods devastated Easton, Kansas, in northwest Leavenworth County. Floodwaters invaded 150 homes and 58 mobile homes in this small, tight-knit community, and Easton Grade School had eight feet of standing water. Lansing Correctional Facility inmates were dispatched to assist in the cleanup of the flood damage. (Courtesy of LCF.)

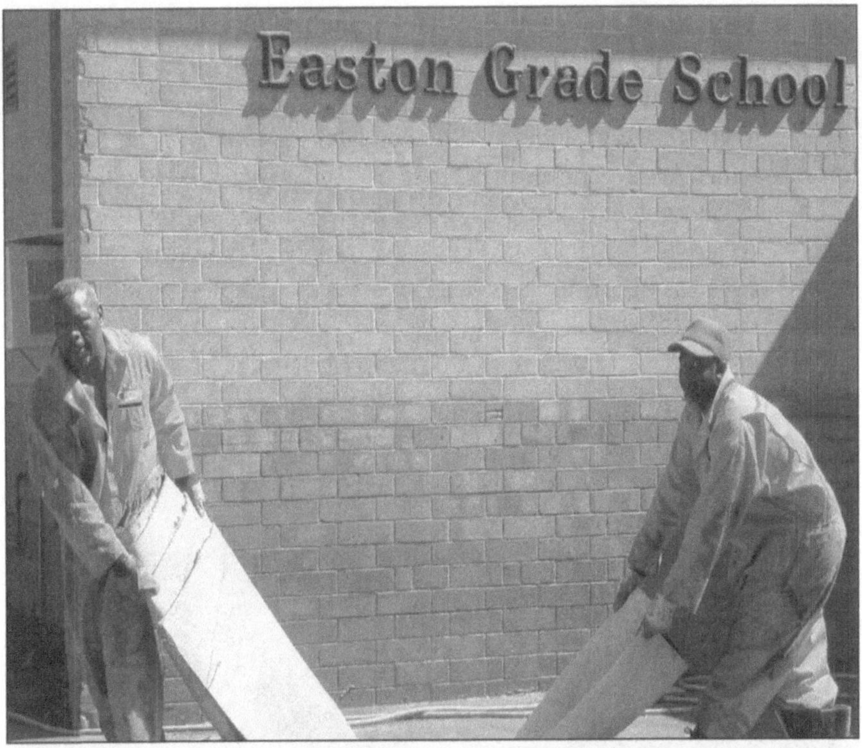

Easton Grade School

Over the years, the Lansing Correctional Facility and the city of Lansing have worked together on a variety of projects, one of which allowed inmates to work for city departments, such as Parks and Recreation or Wastewater. The city benefited from the additional help and labor cost savings. In return, the inmates gained job experience they could use upon release. Although the city of Lansing does not currently employ any inmates within its departments, the inmates assist with preparation and cleanup for city events. The inmates also stained the Lansing Historical Museum's deck. The only costs the city incurred during the project were the supplies.

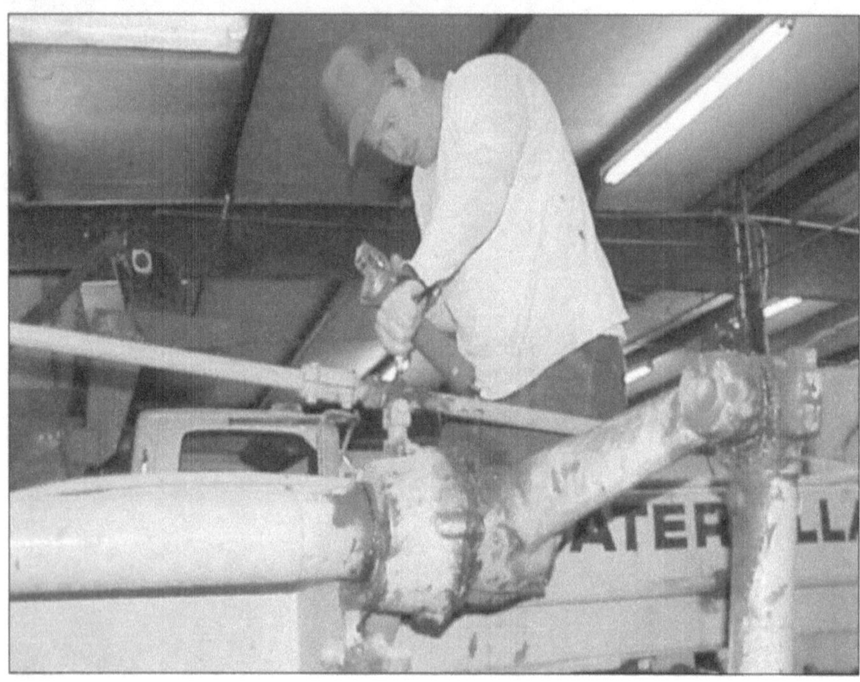

Warden David McKune presents a $10,000 check to Buck O'Neil (center) and director Don B. Motley (right) of the Negro Leagues Baseball Museum in Kansas City, Missouri. Once a month, inmates are allowed to purchase a catered meal from outside the walls. As a way for the inmates to give back to the community, a small fee is added to the meal and put in an account to benefit nonprofits of the warden's choice. (Courtesy of David McKune.)

In 2007, a Chinese delegation visited the Lansing Correctional Facility for a tour with warden David McKune (center). The Lansing Correctional Facility gives tours of the institution to local leadership classes and college students from across the state. The students are usually majors in criminal justice, sociology, psychology, or law enforcement. (Courtesy of David McKune.)

The Lansing Correctional Facility firing range gives individuals an opportunity to practice firing their weapon. The following groups also use the range: Kansas Department of Corrections special enforcement officers, Lansing Police Department, Leavenworth Police Department, Veterans Administration Police Department, and Corrections Corporation of America, Leavenworth, as well as the US Army on occasion. (Courtesy of LCF.)

The Lansing Correctional Facility has a helicopter pad located behind the Lansing Historical Museum on the western edge of the property. Here, a Kansas Highway Patrol helicopter lands at the prison in May 2012. The helicopter was requested by a local law enforcement agency to assist with a case. (Author's collection.)

In appreciation of his service to LCF and the community, warden David McKune (atop the sign) was thanked on the Lansing Pride sign. Located on prison grounds, the sign promotes events in the community, free of charge. Peering out from behind the sign is his administrative staff (from left to right): Chuck Phillips, Dave Ferris, Bill Shipman, Colette Winkelbauer, Brett Peterson, Kyle Deere, Rob Arnold, Cathy Higley, Ron Baker, Rex Pryor, and Jim Collins. (Courtesy of Phil White, LCF.)

After 38 years with the Kansas Department of Corrections, Lansing Correctional Facility warden David McKune (left) shakes hands with KDOC secretary Ray Roberts (right) at his retirement ceremony on September 12, 2012. McKune became LCF warden in 1991, and to date, is the longest-serving warden in the facility's history. Today, McKune is the director of the Juvenile Detention Center in Olathe, Kansas. (Courtesy of Phil White, LCF.)

Posing for a photograph at the LCF warden's office are, from left to right, Colette Winkelbauer, deputy warden of operations; Rex Pryor, warden (seated); Shannon Meyer, deputy warden of programs; and Bill Shipman, deputy warden of support services. These four have a combined total of over 100 years of experience in corrections. All of them began their careers in entry-level positions and worked their way to the top of their fields. (Courtesy of Phil White, LCF.)

The Lansing Correctional Facility memorial recognizes staff members who have lost their lives in the line of duty: officer William Owens, died October 6, 1905; officer David Burns, died December 15, 1923; officer Henry Kenega, died June 20, 1954; officer Don Martin, died August 14, 1978; food supervisor Burch Slote, died July 6, 1980; Sgt. Robert Hurd, died October 11, 1981; and officer Mark Avery, died May 23, 1993. (Courtesy of Phil White, LCF.)